〔家在云和山水间〕

张应杭篆刻习作 · 一九八三年夏

张应杭

著

和善之城 云水胜境

云和之"和"的文化学解读

YUNSHUI SHENGJING
HESHAN ZHI CHENG

ZHEJIANG UNIVERSITY PRESS
浙江大学出版社

图书在版编目（CIP）数据

云水胜境　和善之城：云和之"和"的文化学解读 / 张应杭著.
—杭州：浙江大学出版社，2020.12（2021.4 重印）
ISBN 978-7-308-20768-3

Ⅰ. ①云… Ⅱ. ①张… Ⅲ. ①地方文化－文化研究－云和县 Ⅳ.
① G127.554

中国版本图书馆 CIP 数据核字（2020）第 220643 号

云水胜境　和善之城
云和之"和"的文化学解读

张应杭　著

责任编辑	傅百荣
责任校对	黄伊宁
封面设计	杭州隆盛图文制作有限公司
图片摄影	刘海波
排　　版	杭州隆盛图文制作有限公司
出版发行	浙江大学出版社
	（杭州市天目山路 148 号邮政编码 310007）
	（网址 :http://www.zjupress.com）
印　　刷	杭州高腾印务有限公司
开　　本	880mm×1230mm　1/32
印　　张	8
字　　数	150 千
版 印 次	2020 年 12 月第 1 版　2021 年 4 月第 2 次印刷
书　　号	ISBN 978-7-308-20768-3
定　　价	58.00 元

浙江大学出版社市场运营中心联系方式：(0571)88925591；http://zjdxcbs.tmall.com

作者简介

张应杭，笔名张云和、夏雨等。1963 年 9 月 30 日出生于浙江省云和县赤石古镇。现为浙江大学教授。

1979 年于云和中学毕业后考入华东师范大学哲学专业就读。1986 年研究生毕业应聘至浙江大学任教至今。历任教研室主任、系主任、学院副院长等职，曾获浙江大学本科教学一等奖、浙江省优秀青年教师奖等荣誉。出版著述《中国传统文化概论》《论语道论》《审美的自我》等 20 多部，并在《哲学研究》、《人民日报》、*Journal of Business Ethic Education* 等国内外报刊上发表学术论文及理论文章 190 多篇。

主要社会兼职有：华夏文化促进会（北京）首席专家、杭州电视台"应杭说道"主持人等。

梯田日出

卷首语

Introduction

在浙西南有一个美丽的地方，她有一个非常诗意的名字叫云和。

那是我生于斯，长于斯的故乡。

如果你正为整天穿梭于城市里的钢筋水泥森林而烦闷的话，你来云和吧，这里的云水胜境可以让你枕云听水，获得心灵的宁静。

如果你正被无处不在的利己主义或锱铢必较的拜金主义所困扰的话，你来云和吧，这里和善淳朴的民风会让你怦然心动。

长汀水杉

Introduction

卷首语

In the southwest of Zhejiang Province, there lies a beautiful city called Yunhe, which is a poetic place name in Chinese context.

Home is where the heart is. Yunhe is such a place where I was born and grew up.

If you are bored of traveling through the reinforced concrete buildings in the city all day, come to Yunhe. The cloud-and-water environment here allows you to listen to the waters and get the peace of your heart;

If you are troubled by egoism or money worship, come to Yunhe. The kind and honest folk customs here will make you feel inspired.

瓯江帆影

序
Preface

明景泰三年（公元 1452 年），朝廷析丽水县之浮云、元和两乡建县，于两乡地名中各取一字，是谓云和。此后的县域虽有分分合合，但云和之名一直沿用至今。

这是地名学视阈下的云和。

如果从说文解字的旁通别解看，我觉得云和还可被赋予另外的含义：云者，说也；和者，中华传统文化之精髓也。于是，云和这座城市在我这个土生土长的云和人眼中便成了一座"云"中华"和"文化之城。

几百年来，这座城市默默地以"和"文化熏陶和润泽了生息在此的子民。与此同时，这里的子民又以自己的灵性和践行，不断赋予"和"文化以新的内涵。

作为一位从事传统文化教学与研究的大学老师，我常常利用讲学或参会的机会，在国内外的诸多场合讲述着故乡云和这个以"和"为关键词的美丽故事。

一座城就这样与"和"文化结缘了。

农民新村剪影

Preface

序

In 1452 (during the Ming Dynasty) , the imperial court combined Fuyun and Yuanhe [①] to build a new county named Yunhe. Although the county's area was divided and combined for many times later on, the name of Yunhe has been used ever since.

This is Yunhe from the perspective of toponymy.

From the perspective of semantics, I think that Yunhe can be given another meaning. "Yun" (云) means "to explain" and "He" (和) "the essence of traditional Chinese culture". Therefore, as a native,

---

① In ancient China, there was an administrative regional unit called "Xiang" (乡), which is similar to township in English. Fuyun and Yuanhe were this kind of place names.

I would like to interpret Yunhe as a city which explains the concept of "harmony" (和) [①] in Chinese traditional culture.

For hundreds of years, the city has quietly nurtured its people with the "He" Culture. At the same time, the people here continue to give new meanings to it with their own spirituality and practice.

On various occasions at home and abroad, I often tell beautiful stories of my hometown, which are always related to the word of "He".

A city is thus associated with the "He" Culture.

[①] In the language of Chinese, the character "和" whose pronunciation is "He", means harmony and peace, which was seen as the essence of traditional Chinese culture by many scholars.

县城掠影

目录

Contents

Part One/

Part Two/

云水飘渺

上篇

云和之"和",是人与自然之间的和谐。

从文化学的角度解读,这是中华"和"文化中推崇的天人合一之道。在天人之辨中,与西方推崇征服自然的理念不同,中华优秀传统文化历来主张与自然和谐相处、相辅共生,即《齐物论》中所说的"天地与我并生,而万物与我为一"(庄子语)。

置身云和的云水胜境中,我们可以最真切、最直观地感受到这一天人合一的曼妙意境。

——题记

1. 云水胜境是故乡

My Hometown:
A Wonderland of Clouds and Waters

1970 年夏，父亲作为技术骨干从杭州制氧机厂被抽调回云和参与筹建电机厂，我们一家便随父亲回到故乡。因为厂还没有建起来，作为家属的我们自然也就没有家属楼可住。于是，母亲就带着我和弟弟回到了老家赤石。

在古代主要依靠水路交通出行的年代，赤石可谓瓯江上游的一座繁华古镇。相传赤石之名源自江边一大片红颜色的岩壁。这一传说在赤石老码头曾保留的一块刻有"红岩"两字的墙碑上也得到了佐证。

我在赤石小学就读时的班主任是武娟凤老师，她是解放前的师范生，是当时学校里学历最高的老师。武老师教我们语文课。记

扬帆竞发

得她曾给我们布置过一个作文题目叫"我家乡的大溪"①。在母亲要我另辟蹊径的启发下，我以瓯江清晨时常泛起的云雾为描写对象，写过一篇被武老师作为范文朗读的短文。

几十年过去了，这篇作文的具体文字我早已淡忘，但主题却还依稀记得。好像是说这云雾应该是江水升腾而致，而云雾又化为雨水，以涓涓细流的方式从四面八方回到了江水的怀抱。武老师用她那略带口音的普通话声情并茂地给全班朗读了

---

① 其实，发源于浙闽交界仙霞岭的八百里瓯江在流经云和境内时，其正式的称谓是龙泉溪，但赤石当地人却习惯称其为大溪。

我的作文, 朗读完后还认真地给予了点评。武老师对我的想象力给予了很高的评价。事实上, 那是母亲指点的结果。可因为虚荣心作祟我却没好意思当场申明。

很多年后, 我去探望已退休安居在县城园丁新村的武老师时, 她还提起了这篇作文。她不无感慨地对我说, 现在身虽然住在城里, 但心却时常怀恋赤石大溪的云水景致, 尤其是怀恋那木排串串、白帆点点在不时变幻的薄雾萦绕下所呈现出的如诗如画的美景。

在一刹那间, 我觉得我找到了描写云和之"和"在人与自然层面上的一个关键词。这个词就是: 云水胜境!

云水之境

　　自此之后，我一直喜欢用"云水胜境"一词来描述云和的自然景观。因为我觉得相比于"山水家园"这一流行的宣传语，"云水胜境"这一概括无疑更彰显出云和自然景色的个性。事实上，如果做点资料考据，云和地名来源之一的浮云乡，本就是以浮云溪得名。我想，这条瓯江支流估计在以前应该常有云雾飘浮于溪水之上，故名浮云溪。它恰恰从一个侧面印证了自古以来云和就有这一份自然天成的云水胜境。

　　重要的还在于，就山和水而言，神州大地举目望去，名山胜水可谓不计其数，以山水为亮点概括城市宣传口号的也不胜枚举。但如云和的山水那般有云水意境的并不多。这固然是受益于特殊的地理纬度和丘陵地区的造化，但也和世世代代云和人对森林植被和水土的悉心呵护是分不开的。

　　记得有一年暑假，我陪大姨刘蕙仙去石塘镇下属的叶村坪。这是一个依山而建的畲族村。大姨在浙江省委党校文史教研室任教，她一直对畲族文化颇有研究兴趣。因此之故，我们有了这次探寻与郊游兼顾的出行。

　　令人欣喜的是，此行却让我意外地在村子的一处墙上看到了一块《奉县示禁》的珍贵石碑。从有些斑驳的碑文看，石碑立于清咸丰三年（公元 1854 年）。碑文的示禁内容之一是：如果有人盗砍松树、杉树、油茶树、桐子树等，不仅要罚款，而且明令此后不得

行船的船工

再犯,否则就得收监问罪。面对着这块历经岁月洗礼的石碑,我不由地对古人敬畏自然的这一做法肃然起敬。

　　值得欣慰的是,不仅官府有敬畏自然的意识,民间也一样。比如在云和的很多村落,一直有让小孩子认"樟树亲娘"的习俗。有学者考证,这一独特的民俗文化,在畲汉民族中已延续了近千年。先民们认为郁郁葱葱的樟树有灵性,能保孩子健康成长。而为了让"樟树亲娘"能庇护好孩子,村民们自然就必须善待它。于是,这些先民借助于对某一自然物的崇拜,传递的恰恰是热爱自然、保护生态的朴素理念。

　　小时候，外婆还曾和我讲起我从来未见过的外公这方面的故事。外公刘汉琦先生当年是赤石最早与外国人做木炭生意的人。那时候赤石烧制的木炭经瓯江顺流而下，运至温州再出海销往海外。每年无论生意如何火爆，只要销售到 100 担时，他就歇手不做了。外公的理由是："树砍多了，山神会生气的。"时人闻之，莫不肃然起敬，尊称外公为"汉琦先生"。

　　更值得欣慰的是，虽然历经了斗转星移的历史变迁，但这座城的子民却很好地传承了这一善待自然的传统。比如，我曾在一个偶然的机会里看到相关资料记载，说的是在习惯于乱砍滥伐的年代里，赤石乡下属的好几个自然村的村民在村干部的带领下，为保护森林资源不被外地人砍伐而自发地轮流值守，日夜巡山。

瓯江鹭影

其实，这些质朴的村民未必知道诸如天人合一之类的老庄哲学命题，也未必有文人墨客那般的闲暇之心去品味白鹭与帆影交相辉映的诗情画意。他们之所以这样做是因为他们知道：没有了植被，水土就流失了；没有了水土的滋养，人和自然界的万物都会流离失所。

可以肯定地说，现如今的云和能够成为丽水市第一个国家级生态县，并且绿色发展指数列全省第一，被誉为"中国天然氧吧"，无疑是一代又一代生活在这一方水土的人们善待自然，并坚持不懈、久久为功的结果。

云水一色

　　正是因为有了这样一个敬畏与善待自然的历史文化传承，云和的山山水水才特别地显示出与人的亲和性。故乡的这一方水土自古以来便有"洞宫福地"的美誉，我想正是对这亲和性的形象印证。而且，云与水和谐共生，佳境天成，无疑更是给这一亲和性平添了几分"云水萦回溪上路，叠叠青山，环绕溪东注"（苏轼：《蝶恋花》）的美感。

　　我常常想，生活在云水胜境中的我们在感觉幸运和自豪的同时，更应该用心传承好这一敬畏与善待自然的文化传统。

　　否则，我们就会愧对先人，就会辜负这一方水土。

2. "裁云剪水"的长汀沙滩

Changting Beach:
Trimming Clouds and Cutting Waters

在人与自然的关系问题上，西方一直有人类中心主义[①]和非人类中心主义[②]的争论。人类中心主义的基本立场是"人是目的"。

[①] 这是对待自然问题上西方文化长期秉持的一种观点。在这种观点看来，自然界只是客体，唯有人类才是主体。因此，人类的一切活动都是为了满足自己的生存和发展的需要，不能达到这一目的的活动是没有任何意义的。所谓的保护自然也无非是为了让人类更好地从自然那里获得生产和生活资料。从古希腊普罗塔哥拉的"人是万物的尺度"，到近代康德说"人是目的"，再到现代一些学者提出要重构人类中心主义的主张，表明这一西方文化的传统有多么的根深蒂固。

[②] 这是与人类中心主义相对立的一种观点，主要有动物权利论、大地伦理学、生态中心主义等不同的理论形态。它产生的理论背景是20世纪末生态环境日益恶化，诸如空气污染、水资源枯竭、沙漠化加剧等问题迭起。为解决这一全球性的环境问题，它主张改变当下工业社会的发展模式，秉持反增长、反生产、反技术，崇尚"回到丛林去"之类的立场。

也就是说，在这些持人类中心主义立场的人看来，人类为了生存和发展之目的，可以将自然作为实现目的之手段。可正如我们看到的那样，这一错误的理念直接导致了诸如伦敦雾霾使 1200 多人丧命、洛杉矶光化学烟雾使大量居民患上眼睛痛、呼吸困难的"洛杉矶病"、墨西哥湾的漏油事件对海洋生态的破坏至今无法修复等生态危机的频繁出现。

于是，为了应对和解决生态危机，非人类中心主义的理论应运而生。这一理论在反思欧洲文明征服自然论之弊端的基础上主张"自然是目的"，认为人类要不惜以零增长甚至是负增长来保护好生态环境。但是，秉持人类中心主义立场的人反诘说：保护自然不是为了人类更好地生存和发展吗？如果人的生存和发展都不顾及了，那岂非本末倒置？

在西方，人类中心主义与非人类中心主义就这样从 20 世纪争论到了 21 世纪。迄今为止，好像谁也说服不了谁。

中国传统文化中的天人合一之道显然可以为摆脱人类中心主义和非人类中心主义各执一端的偏执提供新的思路。就云和的个案来看，这一思路可以用八个字描述："裁云剪水，因和而美"。

如果做点词源的考据，"裁云剪水"语出明代诗人屠隆："名擅雕龙，诗成倚马，清思裁云剪水"（《彩毫记·夫妻玩赏》）。可见，古人以"裁云剪水"这个成语来形容诗句构思精妙新奇，我们则借其意指谓人对自然的利用和改造。也就是说，人的生存和发展是必须要从自然界中获取必要的生活资料的。这一点无可厚非。面对着自然界不取不获，拱默不为，人类就将无法生存。西方的非人类中心主义者无视这一基本事实显然是不合理的。

事实上，面对自然界，"裁云剪水"无疑是人的本性。就云和而言，古代农耕文化时代开垦梯田、船帮行船过滩时的巧夺天工，是"裁云剪水"；现代紧水滩水库的发电机组、云和湖里的鱼苗投放、云遮雾绕处的云和雪梨改良和黑木耳、香菇的人工培植，也是"裁云剪水"。

可见，从"裁云剪水"这一立场而论，非人类中心主义的立场是站不住脚的。

但是，就人与自然的关系而论，"裁云剪水"的巧夺天工也罢，精妙匠心、精湛技艺也罢，它不是反自然的恣意妄为，而是遵循着与天地自然"和"为上与"和"为美的原则。正是由此，在"裁云剪水"的基础上我们更应该坚守"因和而美"的立场。

从"因和而美"的原则与立场来看，人类中心主义不顾及自然生态的保护、对自然缺乏敬畏之心也是荒谬的。问题的关键还在于，实践是检验真理的标准。正是依据"裁云剪水，因和而美"这样的乡村治理思路，长汀沙滩不仅应运而生，而且迅速地成为云和旅游的网红景点。

云和的旅游宣传片是这样介绍长汀沙滩的：

这是一个由"山里看海"金点子打造的一个旅游度假村。这里的群众因千米人造沙滩而致富，也因沙滩而成名。这是乡村振兴的成功典范，更是游客们来云和旅游必去的网红打卡点。

其实，在长汀成为如今云和的旅游热门景点之前，我曾经于1988年的暑期去过一次。

当时是陪我在华东师大哲学系读研究生时的导师张天飞教授旧地重游。张老师是杭州人，他年幼便因父亲亡故而和母亲一起随姐姐一家生活。1937年底，在杭州被日寇攻陷后，他随在省政府任职的姐夫一家到了云和。他的童年时代是在抗战时的云和度过的。不幸的是，张老师的母亲没能等到抗战胜利便在云和因病离世了。张老师依稀记得母亲当年就安葬在长汀附近一座邻水的小山岗上。退休之后的张老师一直想重回旧地祭奠母亲。于是，便有了我们师生俩的那次长汀之行。

那时候，整个长汀村给我的印象是非常的破旧不堪。

旧貌换新颜的长汀沙滩之所以特别值得我们赞赏，那是因为长汀人在穷则思变的过程中，没有去掠夺自然资源，甚至都没有去打破大自然的和谐与宁静。村民们无非是在水波平缓、常有雾霭泛起之处"裁"出一方景致，在参差不齐地堆满鹅卵石的河滩上"剪"

长汀假日即景

出一块比较空旷之地，轻轻地覆盖上了一层从海边运回来的沙子。就这样，昔日无人流连的河滩地便被打造成云遮雾绕的山里看海处。它堪称是"裁云剪水，因和而美"的现代杰作。

　　同行的电视台记者还给我透露了一个秘密：这个"山里看海"的金点子出自县委书记叶伯军本人。据说当时不看好这一项目的人还为数不少。但建成后的事实胜于雄辩。我想，这完全应该成为乡村治理中思路决定出路的一个经典案例。

　　而且，与海边的沙滩伴着惊涛骇浪不同，长汀沙滩是那种与湖，与山，与雾霭和谐相处的宁静之美。

　　记得当代诗人海子曾有"我有一所房子，面朝大海，春暖花开"的著名诗句描写他理解并向往的幸福生活。不经意间，长汀人已经令人无比羡慕地拥有了这样的生活。

　　那一天，我们一行人在完成了长汀沙滩所有的拍摄任务之后，却久久地不愿意离去。

长汀水杉

俯瞰长汀

3. 云水相映的云和梯田

Yunhe Terraces with Clouds and Waters
Adding Radiance to Each Other

与长汀沙滩相比，云和梯田显然更是云和旅游的代表性景点。

我有一位就职于杭州师范大学的好友利用到丽水学院讲学的机会，想去云和一游。但他只有半天的空闲时间，要我推荐云和最值得去的一个景点。我毫不犹豫地推荐了云和梯田。我告诉他，人与自然的和谐在云和梯田得到最优雅也是最完美的展示。

的确，被国外旅游和摄影权威刊物评为"中国四十个美景"之一的云和梯田，伴着云海、竹林、溪流、瀑布、雾凇以及古朴的村落等景观，构成了一幅人与自然和谐共生的绝美风景。而且，这一绝美风景和着自然的节拍，四季各不相同，令人叹为观止。

云和梯田的春夏秋冬

来云和梯田的游人，如果恰巧又遇上一年一度的云和梯田开犁节，那他不仅会为"中国最美梯田"的绝美景色而陶醉，也会为这一天人和谐景象背后的古代智慧而折服。

可令我多少有些尴尬的是，我的这位好友在游玩了云和梯田后的当晚就在电话里向我抱怨说，这梯田的景色让他感觉很一般。在他看来：论面积，云和梯田比不了云南的元阳梯田，后者形状各异的梯田连绵成片，每片面积多达上千亩；论色彩斑斓，云和梯田则比不了江西婺源的江岭梯田，每逢春暖花开时节，登高远望江岭万亩梯田，黄灿灿的油菜花与远山近水、白墙黛瓦相映成趣，构成一幅天人合一的精美画卷。通话的最后他问了我一个问题："云和梯田究竟美在何处？"

是啊，这一"中国最美梯田"究竟美在何处呢？2018年的暑假，我带着这个问题向曾经拍出了无数梯田美景的云和融媒体中心摄影记者刘海波讨教。这位有着中国摄影家协会会员头衔的资深记者道出了其中的奥秘：云和梯田的独特之美在于它呈现的是云水相映的精美画卷。尤为神奇的是，这一精美画卷每时每刻都在变幻色彩，令人目不暇接。

见我一副茫然的神态，刘海波便盛情邀请我与他去实地体验一番。我自然是欣然应允。我们约定第二天清晨5点左右在梯田的观景平台见。

虽然曾陪友人、陪同事、陪外国留学生，无数次地去过故乡的这一代表性景点，但我不得不承认唯有这一次才让我真正领略了云和梯田独特的绝美风景。

那天，当我们在梯田的最高观景平台见面时，四周笼罩着浓浓的雾，能见度也就十几米左右。我正担心这四周化不开、挥不走的浓雾会影响对梯田的观赏时，只见一道霞光从远处的云端里缓缓泛出。霞光中，刚刚还浓得仿佛永远化不开的雾，竟然如曼妙的轻纱从身边飘然而去。抬眼望去，灌满水的层层梯田如一面面镜子，把在云层中折射过的霞光映衬得绚丽无比。

伴随着渐渐明亮起来的霞光，雾岚不断飘浮着，并升腾为片片云霭。不一会儿，这些亦雾亦岚亦云亦霭的白色精灵，自近而远、自下而上、自低而高，飘向远处的村落，与袅袅的炊烟汇成了云之和的曼妙景色。

云水胜境在此时此刻得到了最美的展示和诠释。

不仅如此，令我惊喜不已的还在于，到了中午这梯田的云水景色又与早上迥然相异。如果说早上的云霭投映在水中的基调是红褐色，那么到了中午时分，朵朵镶嵌在碧空中的白云，投映在银镜般的梯田中满是耀眼的雪白色。那是纯净得没有一丝杂色的雪白。到了傍晚，在无数块形状各异的水面上呈现出的云，又变幻为片片金红色的朵朵祥云，饱满而高贵。

日出时的梯田

春耕中的梯田

云雾下的梯田

晨曦里的梯田

这一天的行程就在这对绝美的云水胜境的沉醉中度过。有一刹那间,我觉得以前读过的那些诗词佳句,如"云中谁寄锦书来"(李清照:《一剪梅》)"澹然心寄水云间"(朱敦儒 :《鹧鸪天》)"倩谁闲寄水云乡"(韩淲:《浣溪沙》)"渡水穿云心已许"(黄庭坚:《青玉案》),仿佛都成了云和梯田这一云水胜境的绝妙注解。

同行的刘海波告诉我,云和梯田的云水景色不仅一天中变幻多姿,一年四季里更是呈现出春夏秋冬的不同景致。但这些不同的景致却有着一个绝妙的共同点:看云时,水在云下;看水时,云在水中。游人置身其间,绝对可以忘却尘世间因功名利禄而带来的烦恼,让心自由自在地放飞在澄明通透的云水之乡。

我想,这大概就是大自然之于人类的神奇之处。这也是现如今的人们越来越热衷于逃离由钢筋水泥构筑的城市而投向大自然怀抱的缘由。

因为向自然的回归,就是向美的回归。

4. "十里云河" 皆美景

Where There Are Rivers and Clouds,
There Is Beauty in Yunhe

记得 1979 年我怀揣着一纸录取通知书去上海华东师范大学报到的时候，曾向在火车站接待新生的学兄介绍自己来自浙江云和。学兄热情地回答说："噢，很有诗意的两个字。邓丽君有首歌就叫《云河》。原来真的有这样的地方呀！"

多年之后，当我在宣传云和旅游的网页上看到"十里云河"的称谓时，一下子就勾起我对这一往事的回忆。据说"十里云河"的创意出自云和文化名人——陈惠民。这位当年的北大才子因为那个极左年代的错误被发配到云和的乡下教书，但他却称这是个"美丽的错误"。因为自此之后，他把云和视为自己的第二故乡。在教书育人的同时,他经年累月地以研究云和文化为使命,在为云和的文化教育事业做出了杰出贡献的同时,也得到了云和人民对他的尊敬。陈老师获得过很多荣誉称号,最近的一次是在 2019 年的世界丽水人大会期间,他被评为"云和封面人物"。

我觉得陈老师"十里云河"这一概括太精妙了,寥寥数语就把八百里瓯江在云和境内的独特景致精准而浪漫地描绘出来了。

沿着瓯江顺流而下,"十里云河"始于因紧水滩电站筑坝而成的云和湖,蜿蜒十里至与丽水莲都接壤的规溪而终。其间点缀着仙宫水上乐园、慧云禅寺、石浦花海、长汀沙滩、帆影小顺、水墨规溪等风景点。这些景点沿着秀美的瓯江逶迤而来,不断地呈现出云水胜境的一幅幅美丽画卷。

云和湖无疑是"十里云河"景区里最值得推荐的地方。在平整如镜的湖面上,共长天一色的点点帆影,伴着移民新村的泥墙黛瓦、夹岸而生的雪梨花和怡然自得的水鸟,无不向游客诠释着何谓天人合一的审美意境。

云和湖于我这个游子而言,还有着更深的一层关联,那就是湖下那片静谧、沉寂的土地是生我养我的地方——赤石。

前文已略有提及,赤石是一座典型的临江而建的江南古镇。在

云和湖景

主要依靠水路通衢的年代, 它曾经人口繁多, 商贾云集。它供往来船舶停靠的码头就有八个之多, 码头两旁则是一字排开的吊脚楼。每逢夏日的夜晚时分, 沐着凉爽的江风, 趴在吊脚楼的"美人靠"上呆呆地看船来船往, 或听大人说《三国》、讲《水浒》、道《西游》, 绝对是我童年时光里的一桩美事。

后来, 因为建造紧水滩水电站, 这座古镇在 1986 年 6 月 24 日这一天不复存在了。和许多赤石人一样, 我把这一天铭刻在了记忆深处。正是这一天, 紧水滩水库的大坝开始蓄水发电了。从此, 赤石古镇成了我们这些游子乡愁里抹不去的一个记忆。

有一年暑假, 我带自己任教的浙江大学国际学院的三十多位留学生游云和湖, 自然要给学生讲讲我那些沉没在湖底的童年往事。我发现, 有个叫马克的美国男孩却充耳不闻, 只顾看着岸边的山峦发呆。

后来, 我与马克细聊之下才知道, 他是被雨后初晴的半山腰上的一簇簇云霭所吸引。

这位在纽约大都市里长大的美国男孩, 从没有如此近距离地见过云霭。他问我这些云霭是从何而来。我告诉他, 既有植被上的露水蒸发的水汽凝结而成, 也有湖面上腾起的一片片雾霭飘浮而成。片刻之后，他异常兴奋地告诉我他终于知道云和湖为什么叫云和湖了！他告诉我，这"和"应该是 and 之意。也就是说，云和湖应该是"云"和"湖"。马克说他要强烈地建议云和分管旅游的官员，在导游讲解词里应该告诉游客：这里讲述的是一个来自大自然的关于云霭与湖水如何和谐共生的美丽故事。

我在为马克中文功底叹服的同时，更欣赏他的想象力。后来，当我在浙大一个培训班上遇见来自云和文化与旅游局的一位学员时，我很认真地把马克的发现说给他听。我说这的确应该而且可以成为云和湖旅游的一个讲解亮点。因为这个云与湖的故事不仅契合了云和湖的字面意思，而且更充分的理由还在于，正是它让云和湖具备了有别于西湖、洞庭湖、镜泊湖的特质。

烟雨石浦

规溪天桥

　　重要的还在于, 这个特质正是"十里云河"之关键词"云河"两字的精义之所在。事实上, 在"十里云河"的主要景点中, 不仅云和湖是云与湖勾勒出的水墨画, 其他景点中无论是仙宫景区的水上乐园, 还是紧水滩大坝声震天籁、气势恢宏的泄洪之水; 无论是与湖光山色为伴的慧云寺, 还是"裁云剪水"的长汀沙滩; 无论是"白帆点点水云处"的小顺, 还是穿云激水的船帮栖息地石浦与规溪, 都与云水二字有着剪不断的美丽勾连。

又见帆影

尤其因为从水库底层的水轮机组缓缓流出的水几乎是恒温的，于是在春夏秋冬的不同季节便会因温差而生成或浓郁或清淡的雾霭奇观。它把"十里云河"沿溪的两岸妆点得犹如阆苑仙境。一时间，引得全国各地的摄影家纷至沓来。这些作品在屡屡得奖的同时，也使云和的云水胜境让更多的人知晓和称羡。

我想，这应该正是我为什么执着地主张用"云水胜境"来概括和宣传云和全域旅游的原因。

有意思的是，这一份云水胜境也可助力经营效益的增长。在"十里云河"起点处的云和湖上，有一家宋城云曼酒店。因其入住价格不菲等原因，被某旅游网站及一些游客称为"中国的马尔代夫酒店"。我一直觉得这么昂贵的酒店应该不会有太高的入住率。有一次，我一位 EMBA 学生慕名想入住却被婉拒而不得已求助于我。一番打探之后，我告诉他我也爱莫能助，因为那一晚的酒店确实客满了。这事曾经让我颇为惊讶。

后来，我在杭州的一次联谊会上遇见了酒店的投资者黄巧灵，便向他讨教其中的缘由。他很骄傲地告诉我，自己的酒店贵就贵在独一无二的湖光山色。我不解地反问："湖光山色不是很多酒店也有吗？"他答："宋城云曼的湖光山色不仅有山有水，更有湖面上不时泛起的片片云雾，宛如阆苑仙葩。"我顿时恍然大悟。

是啊，习惯宅居在城里的现代人，蓦然间见到了"落日在烟树，云水两空濛"（周紫芝：《水调歌头》）的美景，岂能不动心呢。

这大概就是云曼酒店最吸引人眼球的地方。

云栖木屋

　　不过，相比有些张扬地矗立在湖中间的云曼酒店，我其实更欣赏静静伫立在湖边山坡上的云栖木屋。

　　云栖木屋源自赤石乡党委、乡政府发展农村集体经济，改善民生的初心。它由18栋独立的木屋错落而成。木屋群不仅被500多个品种的玫瑰浪漫地簇拥，而且，每一栋木屋均被设计成面朝湖水的格局。入住的游客凭栏而立，秀美的云和湖便尽收眼底。于是，近处的鲜花与远处的湖光山色，便打造出了现代版的世外桃源。木屋的经营承包者是我赤石的小老乡——练巧忠。这位在云和玩具界业绩颇为骄人的青年企业家，怀揣报效家乡的感恩之心于2015年回到故乡赤石用心经营起了这家远近闻名的网红主题民宿。

　　　　　　　　　　　　　　　　湖光秋色

　　令我特别佩服的是，练巧忠将木屋极其贴切地取名为"云栖"。试想一下，那一缕缕从云和湖中升腾而起的云霭，栖居在木屋的周围，甚至在不经意间就飘进了你的窗户，萦绕在你的身旁。当你靠近窗台，想去触摸飘进来的缕缕云霭时，你又会惊喜地发现，俯瞰中的云和湖湖面宛如一面镜子，把云天树木揽入自己的一泓碧波里。一时间，以湖中的水平面为界，出现了清洌洌的两个对称的云天树木，它们相互倚存，如庄周梦境，似真似幻。

　　于是，自然界的云水胜境便转换成人生的云水美景了。那是一种多么曼妙、多么富有诗意的人生景致啊。

5. 白鹤尖的云海奇观

The Wonderful Sea of Clouds at
Baihejian Mountain Peak

  2019 年暑假，为了更好地在世界丽水人大会期间宣传和展示云和的好山好水，应县委统战部的邀请，我出任了宣传片中的形象大使一职。片子由云和电视台的副台长陈伟飞负责统筹。拍摄间隙，我向她讨教倘若从云与水的视阈去解读云和的自然景色，最有代表性的云水胜境有哪些时，她在列举了云和梯田、云和湖、长汀沙滩后，特别地推荐了白鹤尖。

  陈伟飞告诉我，那是一个异常美丽，真真切切可以用宛如仙境这四个字来描述的地方。

  于是，带着对白鹤尖仙境的美美期待，我们课题组一行驱车前往白鹤尖。因为事先做过功课，我们知道这是云和境内的最高峰，它海拔 1593 米，与牛头山（海拔 1297 米）、灵漈山（海拔 1249 米）、鹿角尖（海拔 1166 米）并称云和四大名山。白鹤尖因山峰像一只白鹤，且山上岩石全为白色而得名。作为地道的云和人，我虽一直闻其名但却从未登临。

不过，对于陈伟飞描述的宛如仙境的白鹤尖云海奇观，我内心是有些疑惑的。我从教三十多年，因为生性的喜好和五湖四海讲学的便利，领略过太多的云海奇观了。比如，就说以云海为主要观赏特征的黄山，我甚至有五上黄山的经历，颇有些"黄山归来不看云海"的自负。

虽然揣着这样一个小小的疑惑，我还是和大家一样在帐篷里早早地躺下了。因为第二天清晨，大家约定要早起去守候或见证云海中磅礴日出的那一壮美时刻。此行的我们显然非常期待这一份美丽的遇见。

令大家惊喜不已的是，我们提前邂逅了白鹤尖云海的美丽。

那天清晨，离预告的日出时刻还早，满怀期待的大家就纷纷钻出了帐篷。风有点大。四周布满了随着山峦起伏而错落有致的风力发电基桩。这些发电基桩在晨曦中闪着银白色的光，不仅丰富着白鹤尖的白色基调，也给四周的景致带来了浓郁的现代化气息。

蓦然间，一片片浓稠且湿润的像雾霭又像云烟的白色精灵，裹挟着马尾松和杜鹃花的清香，朝我们扑面而来。仿佛只要挥一挥手，我们就可以把云海美景拽进怀里。就在我们的一片惊叹声中，只是一刹那间，它们又迅速地随风消散而去，甚至让我们怀疑前面那一刻被云雾缭绕的场景是虚幻的。可还没容我们细细去分辨究竟置身于真实还是虚幻世界时，这些白色精灵又朝我们浓墨重彩地款款袭来。

一时间，云霭就这般来来往往，令人应接不暇。

就这样，在那个清晨我们与云海有了近在咫尺的美丽遇见，似真似幻，且周而复始。

特别值得一提的是，我发现白鹤尖的云，除了观赏原来还可以倾听。也许是因为离阵阵袭来的云雾太近的缘故，只要你用心倾听，会有轻柔的丝丝声在耳边萦绕。那真的是绝妙的天籁之声。我甚至遐想，下山后我应该去有关部门建议在这里建一个亭子，名字就叫"听云轩"。如果能有幸再被邀请给亭子拟副对联，那我就写上：层层叠叠上远山看花开花落，时时刻刻在雾里望云卷云舒。

不久，置身云雾缭绕仙境中的我们，终于迎来了气势恢宏的白鹤尖日出。

白鹤尖的日出、云瀑、杜鹃

　　与黄山日出不同，白鹤尖的日出是在无边无际的瀑布云中出场的。那一望无际、犹如倾倒的瀑布般的云海，被初升的太阳先是染成了红色，再慢慢地染成橘黄色，最后则变成了金黄色，闪烁着佛光般的绝美色彩。难怪有网友在某旅游网站上留言说："看云海不用去黄山，看佛光无须去峨眉，白鹤尖全有！"此言的确不虚。

　　欣赏完了一望无际的云海铺垫出的壮美日出，我们开始了漫无边际的溜达。

　　不经意间，同行中有人在山巅一隅发现了一座石头垒成的小庙，四周摆满了香烛等祭品。据替我们开车兼做向导的师傅说，这是八大仙的神位。每逢干旱了，周边七里八乡的村民来求雨时，它总是特别灵验。我们当中随即有人上网查询，发现这座小庙原来还是颇有来历的。据清同治年间编纂的《云和县志》记载："白鹤峰在县西三十五里，俗呼梅九尖，西山之最高者。上有井泉，祷雨辄应。"

　　以现代科学的立场来看，神灵的保佑或灵验一类的说法自然不可信。但是，我觉得在雾霭如此丰盈、云海如此壮观之地，求雨的概率自然会是很高的。记得以前有首流行歌曲的歌词里就有这么一句："风中有朵雨做的云。"因为从气象学上说，云本就是雨构成的。雨在天为云，云落地则为雨。古人"祷雨辄应"的记载，被我这么一解释，众人有拍手称是的，也有将信将疑的。

　　回城的途中，大家有些疲倦了，纷纷打起了瞌睡。我怕司机受影响，便与其一路聊天借以给他提神。

　　令我惊讶的是，年轻的司机居然知道这首《风中有朵雨做的云》，而且知道唱红这首歌的歌手叫孟庭苇。他告诉我，这首歌是他母亲的最爱，他耳濡目染自然也就很熟悉了。于是，我俩便轻轻哼起了这首歌，"风中有朵雨做的云，一朵雨做的云；云的心里全都是雨，滴滴全都是你……"

　　突然地就想到，这首歌的歌词与白鹤尖的云，白鹤尖的雨，白鹤尖的风，在意境上倒是颇为契合。

　　我不由地感叹，世间的事有时候就是这么奇妙。

白鹤尖祥云

6. 云水发端处——夏洞天

The Start of Clouds and Waters-
Xiadongtian

　　云和的云水胜境又岂止在梯田，岂止在十里云河，岂止在云曼酒店和云栖小屋，岂止在白鹤尖。在云和与龙泉交界处的麻垟村，也隐藏着这样一个云水美景——夏洞天。这是一个外地游客来游览云和山水时，常常会忽视的景点。

　　关于夏洞天曾有一个美丽的传说。据上文提及的《云和县志》记载：有一柳姓女子在溪边洗衣服时，一时好奇误吞了水中拾得的龙卵。孕育三年后她生下龙子。龙子渐渐长大后，一日携母飞抵赤石麻垟的一处深潭成仙而去。啧啧称奇的村民自此称该潭为柳姑潭，称该地为仙人洞。后来，村民们还自发集资修建了龙母宫。

夏洞天瀑布

　　这便是夏洞天的由来。据史料记载，那句"云和出真龙，龙母在赤石"的谚语在清同治年间便开始在民间流传。

　　神话毕竟是神话，自然当不得真。1992年的暑期，时任浙大人文学院副院长的我因为分管的工作中包括工会旅游一项，便组织了一次部分教职工的云和游。当游至夏洞天谈及龙母的神话传说时，我们中文系一位研究民间神话的老师解释说，对腾云驾雾、呼风唤雨之龙的诸多传说往往都出自江河湖海之畔的民间，这正好证明了神话传说其实是有着现实生活影子的。据此，他认为在云和这么好的云水之地如果没有关于龙的传说才是不可思议的。

那一天，原本习惯于正襟危坐的老师们一反常态，大家在柳姑潭戏水、打闹，在龙母宫边上垒灶做饭，用夏洞天清冽的泉水泡杭州带过来的龙井茶……我们度过了异常开心、自在、欢悦的一天。

今年夏天重游夏洞天的我们在返程途中，正是晚霞布满天际时分。红彤彤的云霞倒映在水田里，与远处的几缕袅袅炊烟交相辉映，很有几分魏兰①先生"烟村三两家，几处互云霞"（魏兰：《过独屿岭》）诗句描写的意境。

而且，此刻雨后阳光乍现的夏洞天，水是灵动的，水面上升腾的雾霭是流动的，甚至穿过密林那斑斑点点的阳光也随着清风起舞的枝干和叶片而美美地晃动着。唯有山静静地矗立着。面对着这一幅动静相宜的自然美景，蓦然间，袁枚的诗句便浮现在我脑海里："雨过山洗容，云来山入梦；云雨自往来，青山原不动。"（袁枚：《无题诗》）

这是我很喜欢的一首古诗。此前一直不明白为什么在那么多古诗词当中独独偏爱此诗。在夏洞天的此时此刻，我找到了答案：因为它总能撩拨起我对故乡云水地的那一缕浓郁的乡愁。

① 魏兰（1866—1928），字石生、号浮云，浙江云和人。曾是光复会领导人之一，为辛亥革命先行者。辛亥革命后，他积极发展实业，对云和雪梨大规模种植并使其成为驰名品牌贡献尤大。1928年9月17日在家病逝，其墓在云和镇南五里之南山。有《浮云集》《畲客风俗》《魏氏诗集》等流传后世。

雾里看竹

云中揽胜

进香古道

不仅如此，这首诗还触发我的灵感，我仿佛一下子找到了云水胜境的源头：那潭中不断泛起的氤氲，升腾为弥漫的云烟，飘飘荡荡地散落在丛林之间，回绕在层层叠叠的山峦之巅，云遮雾绕的"云"景由此发端；那清洌洌的潭水，即便是干旱少雨时节也能源源不断地流出溪谷，以涓涓细流汇成了八百里瓯江的波澜壮阔，桃花流水的"水"境由此发端。

也是由此，我一下子理解了王维为什么会有"行到水穷处，坐看云起时"（王维：《终南别业》）的诗句流传后世。后人习惯将其演绎为人生无须害怕山穷水尽，只要心态好自然会有云兴霞蔚、彩虹贯日的好时光。我倒觉得这一诗句也许就是诗人流连山水时对云与水的一种自然和本然的描绘。事实上，用这两句诗描写眼前夏洞天的云与水可谓最贴切不过。

沿着蜿蜒的古道，依依不舍地离开夏洞天时，很有点眼前有景道不出的遗憾。既然道不出，那就借古人的诗来应个景。我在吟了"行到水穷处，坐看云起时"后，课题组的朱晓虹博士也吟了句唐诗："风带泉声流谷口，云和山影落潭心"（释延寿：《山居诗》），引得大家纷纷拍手称妙。

张应杭书法习作：《山居诗》

我常恨自己没有苏东坡那样的名气与才情，如果有，我会像大学士那样以一句"欲把西湖比西子，淡妆浓抹总相宜"（苏轼：《饮湖上初晴后雨二首·其二》）之类的诗来让云和的云水美景闻名天下。同理，我或者如有米芾那样的名士气概和书法功力，一定会模仿他在武当山写上"第一山"[①]那样，在云和湖畔或高速出口找一块巨石，龙飞凤舞地写上"第一云水地"这样几个大字。

我甚至推想，云和人那一份被外人称羡的"灵范"，也许正是云的睿智和水的灵性赋予的。

[①] 在中国有很多气势磅礴的名山，中外驰名，举世瞩目。但对于哪座山堪称"第一山"却一直颇多歧义。有说是泰山，有说是武当山，有说是黄山，有说是华山。

和美之境

下篇

云和之"和"，更是人与人之间的和善。

从文化学的角度解读，这是中华"和"文化中推崇的人我合一之道。在人我之辩中，与西方利己主义的理念以及"他人即地狱"（萨特语）的诅咒不同，中华优秀传统文化历来主张与他者的和谐相处，即《论语》所谓的"君子成人之美，不成人之恶"（孔子语）。

云和崇和向善的乡土文化堪称对这一人我合一之道最具象、最直接的诠释。

——题记

1. 和善包容的云和人性格

The Kind and Inclusive Yunhe People

一方水土养一方人，一方人便有一方人的独特性情。

记得是 2002 年底，我曾经的一位学生到云和县政府任职。在一次聊及云和人性格时，他提及一件很有意思的事：作为外地人因为不会说云和方言，他第一次去菜场时很担心会挨宰。于是，有着高学历背景的他，先是不动声色地旁观摊主与他人的交易，然后再上前买自己看中的恰好刚刚交易过的菜。令他感动的是，卖菜的小贩不仅没有欺生涨价，而且还因担心眼前的小伙子调料不够周全，善意地送了一把小葱给他。

这位昔日的学生进而告诉我，据他观察，云和人的这一和善包容性格不仅体现在菜场里的小贩身上，不仅体现在踏黄包车的车夫那里，也不仅体现在左邻右舍见面时一句善意的"吃了没"的方言问候语，更体现在单位里同事之间关系的融洽、领导对下属的和善，以及师者对学生的和善、医者对患者的和善、为政者对百姓的和善、原住民对外来者的和善，如是等等。

梅湾百家宴

我饶有兴致地问他："那你觉得为什么云和人会有这个性格？"他答："是因为云和的天和、地和、山和、水和的自然环境造就的。正如俗语说的穷山恶水出刁民，那很自然地我们也可以说：好山好水出善民嘛。"

用自然环境来解释云和人性情中的和善包容固然也有几分道理，但仅从自然地理的角度解释显然还是不够的。为什么同样是置身八百里瓯江，云和人就形成了这一性情呢？答案或许更应该从文化学的角度探寻。

我觉得从中华传统文化的传承方面说，山城云和因为地理位置的偏僻，故近代以来没有像一些沿海城市那样深受西学东渐的西方利己主义文化的影响，从而比较好地保存了古代以儒家为道统的崇和向善的优秀传统文化。

文化学家曾经在宏观层面把世界文化划分为三大文化圈①。中国和东亚地区位于儒家文化圈内。儒家文化的核心理念是"仁者爱人"（《论语·颜渊》），它主张将心比心、推己及人的和善伦理。但后来西学涌入，"人对人像狼"（霍布斯语）"他人即地狱"（萨特语）

---

① 文化圈是文化人类学的重要概念之一。这一概念最初是由文化人类学家莱奥·弗罗贝纽斯提出。一般而论，学者们倾向于认为全球有三大文化圈，即基督教文化圈、伊斯兰教文化圈和儒家文化圈。基督教文化圈主要分布在欧洲、美洲、澳洲等地，伊斯兰文化圈主要分布在亚洲西部、南部和北非等地，儒家文化圈主要分布在东亚等地。

"自私的基因"(道金斯语)之类的西方文化强势来袭,严重地误导了一些中国人的做人理念。幸运的是,云和这座偏远山城受到的影响显然没有像一些大都市那样深,那样广。

这是我解释云和人性情为什么和善包容的一个论据。

记得有一年我应邀在云和电视台做一专题节目时,我论及过这一观点。但是,我的同学,同时也是节目总监的王月岳却提醒我仅有这个论据好像是不够的。她举例说,同样是偏僻之地,同样很少受到西方文化的影响,很多地方却民风彪悍,人心不古。可见,还应该有进一步的理由来支撑我的立论。

正是在王月岳的启发下,我找到了云和本土积淀深厚的移民文化作为我立论的补充依据。

众所周知,处州九县(区),唯有云和是移民迁入最多的城市。移民城市因其居民来自四面八方,影响和熏陶其习性的文化自然也是多元的。由此决定了它的居民其内生的性格便往往会呈现出和善包容。我想这应该是解读云和人和善包容之性情更本土化的文化学思路。

欢快的畲家游戏：荡竹梢

从史料记载看，云和的大规模移民就有畲民、汀州人、新安江人的三次迁入。

如今散布在云和各个乡镇的畲族同胞，是至今一千多年前迁徙过来的。他们的原居住地是广东潮州的凤凰山。据史料记载，从唐永泰年间开始便陆陆续续地有畲民迁至云和、景宁一带。当他们多少有些惴惴不安地来到这里时，惊讶地发现这里的原住民热情地把他们称为"客家人"，即远道而来的畲家客人！正是由此，云和的方言中多了一个非常和善的词汇——它叫"畲客人"①。

① 不知从何时何地开始，云和方言中的"畲客人"一语被误认为是对畲族同胞的蔑称。笔者从语义学的角度考证认为，这绝对是个流行的误解。事实上，这应该是云和原住民对外地迁徙而来的畲族同胞的尊称。

如果畲族同胞有自己文字的话，相信一定会用最美的词汇描述出初来乍到云和时内心的那一份感动。

三百多年前，说闽语、行闽俗的福建汀州人也来到了云和。他们同样得到了原住民的悦纳。正是有赖于此，他们得以与原住民和谐相处，以自己的勤劳与智慧在浙西南的这一块土地上安身立命，并成就斐然。

一个有意思的问题是，汀州府是客家人众所周知的发祥地，但与迁往别的地方的汀州人被称为"客家人"不同，在云和的他们却被称为"汀州人"。而且，他们自己也非常乐意接受这个称谓。个中缘由曾让专门研究客家文化的一些专家百思不得其解。其实，答案非常简单：因为云和已经有一支"客家人"（即畲民）先于他们来到了瓯江上游的这片土地安居乐业。于是，为了与此前的"客家人"相区分，他们更愿意称自己是"汀州人"。

这个细节堪称是对云和移民史的形象注解。

20世纪50年代，为了修建第一座中国人自行设计并建设安装的水电站——新安江水电站，约三十万的水库移民需要被安置。那是新中国成立后非常浩大的一项社会工程。

2009年1月，人民文学出版社推出了《国家特别行动：新安江大移民——迟到五十年的报告》一书。作者是一位新安江库区移民的后代。有媒体评论此书说："一段淹没在美丽千岛湖底的沉痛往事，终于浮出了水面。"作者在书中纪实性地还原了一些移民遭遇到诸如劣质的安置房、与接收地居民不断激化的矛盾、望眼欲穿的安置费等问题后，用了一句"三十万浙西人民的悲壮迁徙"来总结那一段历史。我掩卷之际，颇有些心酸。

我在云中就读时的一位好友就是新安江移民。记得是2010年春节回家，我曾与他聊及此书。对这段历史颇有研究兴趣的他坦言，被安置至云和的新安江库区移民是幸运的，因为书中提及的那些辛酸事，至少他们家就没有遇到。他的父亲甚至还娶到了被村民誉为"五朵金花"之一的当地姑娘为妻。

而且，据他了解，云和的新安江移民几乎没有一家被书中描述的问题所困扰。恰恰相反，因为云和原住民的和善，他们很快便融入了云和这一方水土，成家立业，成为了新云和人。

重要的是，在这座城，人和人之间的和善包容又岂止体现在原住民与移民的关系之中呢。

2012年，一个发生在云和梯田景区梅竹村的爱情故事曾被拍成微电影而广为传颂。

盛装的畲族少女

女主人公是位上海某高校的教师，慕名来游云和梯田。结果在短短五天的游览时间里，她在梅竹村遇见了真爱，最终把身和心都留在了云和。正如她对媒体坦言的那样：爱云和的美景，更爱云和人的淳朴、灵性与和善。现如今，男女主人公经营的民宿"云上5天"已成为网红客栈。一时间，全国各地的游客慕名而来，他们除了慕云和梯田之名而来之外，更希望零距离地感受客栈主人这一份浪漫的爱……

2013年，浙江省社会科学院院长、博士生导师万斌教授受邀到丽水讲学。完成讲学任务后，因浙江红色文化研究的需要他去了云和的梅湾村做专题调研。可就在他们一行要返程时，司机发现车发动不了了。这可把万教授急坏了，因为他第二天有个重要会议要主持，当天必须赶回杭州。

见万教授着急万分的样子，一位路过的年轻人自告奋勇地开着自己的私家车把他送到了丽水火车站。这位小伙子是因为参加单位党组织活动而来的梅湾，他与万斌教授素昧平生……

2018年，某知名旅游网站的一个故事也颇有点击率。

发文者是来云和自驾游的温州游客吕先生。他因为途中车坏了，抵达云和时已经是子夜时分。街上的店铺早已打烊。饥饿难忍的他抱着试试看的心情给宾馆老板打了求助电话。结果一刻钟不到，几碗热气腾腾的云和特色面——笋衣鸡蛋面就送到了他及家人面前。老板坦言，自己和家人原本已经睡下了，但他本人也曾有饥饿难忍而辗转难眠的经历，于是便打火起灶做了这几碗面。

这位吕先生后来在朋友圈里说：他生平吃过最美味的面是在云和吃到的，因为那碗面有善良与淳朴做汤料……

在云和，这样的故事几乎每天都有发生。如果我们在电脑网页的搜索引擎中输入"云和好人"这个关键词，马上会跳出无数感人故事的相关链接。

我想，这正是云和人和善包容性格的一种自然呈现。

2. 无处不在的"女神"崇拜

The Ubiquitous Goddess Worship

如果云水胜境是云和随处可见的自然景观的话，那么，无处不在的"女神"崇拜则构成了云和一道颇具地方特色的文化景观。

对云和地域文化颇有研究的陈惠民说，在云和的村村落落遍布着一座座造型不同却香火不断的夫人庙。他精当地把它们统称为"女神"庙。而且，在陈惠民看来，全国各地固然也有林林总总的"女神"庙以及各具特色的女神崇拜现象，但像云和这样形成大规模、集群式的"女神"崇拜却是非常罕见的。

在这些林林总总的"女神"崇拜中,对天妃娘娘(即妈祖)的崇拜无疑最为云和的民众知晓。

据宋代的文献资料记载,妈祖本是莆田湄洲海边一位姓林名默的女子。因出生时一声不哭,为此,父亲给她取名为"默"。有一次,有艘商船经过湄洲时遭到飓风袭击,船底触礁,海水涌进船舱,情况十分危急,船中人哀号求救。林默见状,非常焦急地对村民说:这艘商船即将沉没,应赶快前去援救!

可大家看着眼前的狂风巨浪,因为害怕谁也不敢向前。就在这紧急关头,只见林默信手将脚边小草拽了几根,抛向大海。刹那间,几根小草变成大杉木漂向商船。因有大杉木相附,船终于不再下沉。不一会,风平浪息,船上的人都以为是苍天相助,互相庆贺。待到将船靠岸,却忽然间发现杉木已不知去向。经询问乡人,才知化草成杉的乃是林默的神奇功力。于是,林默的故事便广为传颂。后来,人们亲切地称她为妈祖。

关于妈祖的类似传说不胜其数。她一生在大海中救急扶危,在惊涛骇浪中拯救过许多渔舟商船。更令人动容的是,她立志不嫁,誓以慈悲为怀,专以行善济世为己任。

近一千年间,各个朝代对妈祖的封号多达四十余个。咸丰皇帝曾封妈祖为天后，其封号长达六十四字："护国庇民妙灵昭应宏仁普济福佑群生诚感咸孚显神赞顺垂慈笃佑安澜利运潭覃海宇恬波宜惠导流衍庆靖洋锡祉恩周德普卫漕保泰振武绥疆天后之神"。在清代被封为天后之前，从宋朝皇帝宋光宗诏封妈祖为"灵惠妃"起，其封号有"英烈妃""慈济妃""普济天妃""慈惠天妃"等，故民间更习惯于称妈祖为天妃。

后台中的花鼓戏演员

随着三百年前汀州人的迁入，天妃崇拜也随之进入云和一带。天妃庇护的地方也自然地由大海而延伸到江河湖泊。但不变的是她悲天悯人、普度众生的情怀。

正是由此，几百年来，在云和凡是有江有湖的地方，几乎都有天妃宫或妈祖庙的存在。小时候我常常听外婆讲，现如今沉没于云和湖下的那座由赤石汀州人建造的天妃宫曾经香客盈门，每年正月里给天妃娘娘换衣装的时候，要请戏班子连唱三天三夜花鼓戏以示隆重。如今云和湖上的望乡楼里安置的那口大钟就是从赤石的天妃宫中移上来的。

云和镇解放街街头也有一座天后宫，它建于乾隆年间，曾经朝拜者盈门，香火极旺。今天这座天后宫在汀州人后裔阙松青主持下已修缮一新。修缮后的这座天后宫，除了诸多顶礼膜拜者前来进香外，它也成了云和汀州人联络感情、寄寓乡愁的地方。

事实上，在云和民间不仅有对悲悯助人的天妃崇拜，也还有对孝敬婆母，乐于助人的马夫人（马天仙），对不惜以少女的贞洁名声为代价救人性命的插花娘娘，对勤勤恳恳协助父亲垦荒种植的汤夫人等的崇拜。

这一切恰恰都表明云和本土文化中实实在在地积淀着浓郁的和善精神。

　　正如马克思说的那样:"人创造了宗教,而不是宗教创造了人。"①
这也就是说,宗教的本质就是人的本质。民间的宗教崇拜也当作如
是观。我觉得云和民间大规模集群式地对"女神"的顶礼膜拜,其
本质正是一种道德崇拜,具体地说就是对慈悲、助人、共济等和善
精神的崇拜。

　　特别值得一提的是,在我个人看来,相比于对上帝、真主之类
崇拜而言,对来自现实生活、作为道德化身的"女神"崇拜显然更
具世俗性和亲和力。

　　我想,"女神"崇拜无疑是云和之"和"在和善层面上的一个
生动印证。

① 马克思:《黑格尔法哲学批判导言》,《马克思恩格斯选集》(第
1卷),北京:人民出版社,1995年版,第1页。

解放街的天后宫

3. 名山尽见观音殿

Where There Are Famous Mountains,
There Are Guanyin Temples in Yunhe

如果说对诸如妈祖一类的"女神"崇拜是云和原生态的本土信仰，那么对佛教的信仰则是一种对外来信仰文化的接受。与全国各地一样，云和也存在着诸多的佛教寺庙。

在云和城的东大门，伴着平缓而开阔的浮云溪矗立着一座形如蹲狮的山——狮山。古时候，此山曾列云和八景之冠。山中有寺，称为普仁寺，素有"处州十县朝拜中心"①之誉。作为狮山主体建筑的普仁寺几经沧桑，清道光十四年（公元 1834 年）最后一次重建时，掘得宋代古砖一枚，镌刻有"嘉祐八年"的字样，可见该寺已有千年香火。从历代文人的诗文中可以得知，普仁寺当时是供奉观音②的寺庙，曾经声誉远播。

① 现如今的丽水之域旧称处州十县，除了现在的九县区外，曾经还有一个宣平县，后于 1958 年撤消，它的所属地域分别划归毗邻的武义、莲都、松阳三县区。

② 观音原称观世音，是梵文的意译。其意指这尊菩萨能以大慈大悲之心观听到来自世间需要度脱苦难的所有声音，故称观世音。后来为了避唐太宗李世民的名讳，改称观音。

狮山远眺

　　无独有偶的是，"十里云河"上游的著名景点慧云讲寺也是先有观音殿后有寺院。我曾经与慧云寺的住持寂凡法师聊及该寺前世今生的话题。法师告诉我，现在的慧云寺是众多善男信女发心筹资、十方高僧大德发愿加持于2007年底落成并开光的。

　　据相关史料记载，慧云寺的前身为"官坑观音殿"。三百年来，它一直香火颇盛。民间一句"官坑拜观音"的口头禅印证了这一点。相传，在观音殿后面的岩石上常有老鹰聚在此处聆听梵音，久久不愿离去。年轻而睿智的寂凡法师在某一次与皈依者的交谈时笑称：与其说老鹰在此领悟禅机，还不如说是在这里祈求大慈大悲的观音菩萨保佑与庇护。的确，佛家向来持"众生平等"的教义，因此，在救苦救难的观音菩萨法眼中，其庇护与救助的对象自然包括老鹰在内的一切有情众生。

　　此外，位于崇头镇武岱峰上的武峰寺和沙溪乡后山村的景德寺，也是云和境内著名的佛教寺庙。

慧云寺内观音像

慧云寺外水云天

　　武岱峰上的这座武峰寺曾被称为瑞云庵。据史料记载，自唐代僧人在此建寺后曾吸引着无数的信徒和文人墨客接踵而至。曾参与编撰《云和县志》的清人王树英就曾有《武岱山》诗流传后世："老屋半依竹，闲云时在山；低徊寻古迹，残碣点苔斑"。

　　景德寺也始建于唐代。据民间传说，这座常年香火不断的寺庙之所以叫景德寺，与明代的正德皇帝朱厚照有关。当年微服私访的朱厚照在此遇歹人打劫，幸蒙住持和尚出手相救。皇帝回京后不仅赏金千两以用重修庙宇，还特以年号赐名——正德寺。因为云和话里"正"与"景"同音，便有了尔后的景德寺之名。

武岱峰上武峰寺

这武峰、景德两处寺庙几经毁损和重建，我们今天已经无法确切考证最初是不是供奉观音的道场。不过，迄今为止去烧香的信徒最流行的问候语，不外乎是"请观音菩萨保佑""给观音娘娘还愿"之类的话。

更奇特的是，在著名的牛头山景区，道教的八仙也与佛教的观音菩萨有了关联。作为云和四大名山之一的牛头山位于紧水滩水库东北面，云和、松阳两县的交界处，因主峰耸立霄汉，远观其状似牛头而得名。

关于牛头山自古便有"牛头八面尽见处州十县"之说,可见其登高望远之气势。相传,一位修道者以一己之功,历经数载在牛头山修成了八仙庙,供奉着道教中的铁拐李、汉钟离、张果老、蓝采和、何仙姑、吕洞宾、韩湘子、曹国舅八位得道尊者。可是,当地人却一直称他们为八仙菩萨。每逢观音菩萨生日,或得道日时,进香供花的顶礼膜拜者甚众。

记得有一年的暑假,我与若干友人去登牛头山。当日恰逢农历六月十九日,即相传的观音得道日,但见许多人在八仙庙里非常虔诚地拜观音。我一时兴起,便与其中一位为孩子考大学来求菩萨保佑的中年妇女聊了起来。我问为什么求观音菩萨保佑不去慧云寺却来了八仙庙。她很认真地告诉我:"八仙是观音的八个弟子。求观音的人太多,怕菩萨忙不过来,故求菩萨的弟子也许更有庇护或保佑之功。"听闻此言,我和我的几位同行者禁不住掩嘴而笑。

可见,在云和的云水胜境中,与"女神"崇拜交相辉映的"观音崇拜"也堪称云和地域文化的一道亮丽风景线。

如果说这些原本来自现实生活中的和善女性被百姓顶礼膜拜尚可理解的话,那么这个"观音崇拜"便有些让我费解。众所周知,佛教源自印度,自汉代传入中国。依据印度佛教的义理,拜佛应该比拜菩萨更能获得加持力。[①]但在云和的寺院丛林中,拜观音菩萨的现象却比比皆是。

---

① 在佛教的修行层次上由低到高依次是罗汉、菩萨、佛。也即是说,就佛教的修行教义而言,佛比菩萨的修行阶位要更高,因而其加持力自然更大。

2006 年 4 月 13 日，首届世界佛教论坛在杭州开幕。时任浙江省委书记的习近平曾莅临大会并致开幕词。论坛的后半部分移至舟山的普陀山进行。因为普陀山是观音菩萨的道场，很自然地让作为与会者的我联想起云和佛教寺庙的"观音崇拜"现象。

在一次小组讨论时我提出了自己的疑惑：佛教的修行阶位依次为罗汉、菩萨、佛。这也就是说，观音只是菩萨的阶位，可为什么在云和的佛教寺庙里往往先有观音殿？在民间甚至出现"只知观音不知佛""只拜观音不拜佛"的奇特现象？与会者给出的答案自然是见仁见智，莫衷一是。

2016 年，我应邀去浙江台州参加一个和合文化的研讨会。会议期间安排的一个考察瞬间触动了我的灵感。我蓦然意识到，正如有着和与合文化悠久积淀的台州十里八乡往往供"笑口常开、大肚能容"的弥勒佛那样，云和民间对大慈大悲观音的崇拜，也是因为本土文化中一直有着和善之风的长久传承。

这是善与善的美丽相遇与内在契合。

针对佛教在中国传播中出现的诸如拜观音或拜弥勒的区域性选择情形，曾任中国佛教协会会长的赵朴初先生认为，这是佛教中国化过程中极为普遍的一个现象。这一选择性崇拜的现象可以还原出中华本土文化不同区域的诸多特质。

我终于意识到，云和佛教无处不在的观音崇拜，正是对这一方水土原生的和善文化的形象还原、再现和寄寓。

云水相拥的慧云寺

4. 孝子坊、百岁坊、五代同堂匾的故事

Stories About the Worship of
Filial Piety and Family Love

　　如果说"女神"崇拜中助人为乐的女神和观音崇拜中大慈大悲的观音菩萨，其善心指向的是众生，那么，在云和民间还有一种崇拜对象，其善心是指向特定的个人，比如对父母的孝、对兄弟姐妹的悌、对朋友的忠、对陌生人的信。

　　与全国各地相仿，云和民间也有对孝悌忠信的崇拜。而遍布云和城乡的祠堂便成为这一文化传承和光大的重要场所。

　　当然，这一孝悌忠信文化的传承也还有其它的形式。比如与神州各地一样，云和历史上也有孝子的感人故事载于史册，也曾建有让后人对孝子顶礼膜拜的地方——孝子坊。在云和县城的解放

新建的祠堂

西街就曾有这样一座表彰孝子功德的著名牌坊。这座牌坊主人公的其人其事毫不逊色于《二十四孝》中记载的那些经典故事。

这个故事的历史背景是清康熙十三年（公元 1674 年）福建总兵耿精忠起兵造反。叛军由闽进浙，在占领云和县城后大肆烧杀抢掠，无恶不作。

这时，云和城内有个叫王家较的年轻人挺身而出，联络了一些有正义感的人与叛军对抗。他们以熟悉地形和深得百姓拥戴的有利条件除暴安良，一时间让叛军闻风丧胆。叛军多方搜捕无果之后，居然将王家较的父亲拘捕入狱，并扬言将择日问斩。王家较闻讯后只身闯入叛军大营，愿以自己的性命换回父亲的自由。他还机智地以叛军首领耿精忠的名字为例质问道："以父亲要挟儿子，何以耿直？为一己私利造反，何以精忠？"据说，耿精忠被王家较的大义凛然所感动，最终释放了他们父子。

后人感动于王家较的故事，雍正年间一座孝子坊便于车来人往的街市中矗立起来。听我的大舅舅说，这座孝子坊一直保存至1953年在县城改造时才被拆除。

在云和还有一座建于清道光年间的百岁坊。

百岁坊的主人叫饶玉干。相传五十岁那年，他挑着一担行李到女儿家养老。行李中除了换洗的衣服等生活用品外还有他一辈子的积蓄，如银子、田契、珠宝等。起初，女儿女婿还是挺孝顺的，可日子一长就有些不耐烦了，话里话外开始透出对老人家的嫌弃。

饶玉干老人受不了这口气，择日挑着行李回家了。路上，他

桑岭老屋

遇到一位和善的守寡妇人,不仅帮他挑行李,而且还热情相邀他去自己家喝茶、歇脚。结果两人一见钟情。婚后的他俩不仅相敬如宾,日子过得红火,而且还子孙满堂。这位饶玉干老人一直活到一百岁才辞世。地方官府依据朝廷颁布的条例拨款为他立了牌坊,上书"升平人瑞"四字。当地百姓一直称它为"百岁坊"。

这座古朴典雅的百岁坊原在龙门镇的瑞滩村水口。因紧水滩电站建设,于1996年迁至紧水滩镇的飞凤山公路旁。如果说前些年它还有些孤寂地矗立在那里的话,现如今已成为文化旅游一景。

在云和的文化遗迹中还有一块五代同堂匾也颇值得一提。

五代同堂匾位于石塘镇的桑岭古村。这块匾之所以一直被村民们津津乐道,是因为它向世人诉说着一个关于悌的美德故事。

据考证,桑岭古村落是清康熙年间由江姓太公自汀州迁徙落户而成。在此落户的族人秉承太公孝悌立身、勤俭处世的家训,子孙后代不仅和睦相处,而且出息者颇多。相传康熙皇帝曾赏赐太公龙头拐杖一支以示嘉勉,江姓后人颇引以为豪。族人中有第五代文字辈中的江文潮老人,他与四代子孙共计八十六人同住一个院落里,其乐融融。民国十六年(公元1927年),驻扎云和的第二十六军军长周凤岐为江文潮一家的事迹感动,特意书写了"五代同堂"四字以示敬仰,一时传为佳话。

这块牌匾现如今已经成为桑岭古村的一张亮丽名片。这位题匾者周凤岐乃清末秀才出身,经秋瑾介绍曾加入过光复会,其字还颇有几分书家笔韵。

五代同堂匾

　　重要的还在于，孝子坊、百岁坊、五代同堂匾仅仅只是云和本土文化遗迹的一个缩影。从相关史料记载来看，云和县域内尚有很多类似的表彰和弘扬孝悌忠信美德嘉行的牌坊。时光流变，遗憾的是今天已不复得见，难窥其貌了。

　　世道沧桑本是必然。孝子坊被拆了，百岁坊也被迁移过，五代同堂匾在"破'四旧'"的年代里也曾落满了灰尘。但令人欣慰的是，人与人之间的和善之道，作为云和"和"文化中最重要的内容，正被这座城的人们所代代传承。

　　正是有赖于这一传承，一座城市冰冷的历史才变得有温度。

5. 以忠义彰显家国情怀

A City of Patriotism:
Loyalty and Righteousness

如果说和善之德中的孝悌因其指向的还是父母兄弟等亲人，尚具有某种狭隘性的话，那么，和善之德中的忠义美德则更凸显其普世性。也因此，它更闪烁出和善之德的人性光芒。

从家国关系而言，忠义的本质是追求家与国的和合，或者说是追求小我与大我的和合。在国家需要的时候，能够牺牲小我之家而精忠报国。这是中华民族自古以来就非常推崇的一种家国情怀。

在云和，家国情怀的彰显莫过于中华民族与日寇抗战的那个艰难岁月。

1937年12月杭州沦陷后，浙江省政府决定往浙西南迁徙。这一西迁之路经龙游、永康、松阳一路走来可谓备尝艰辛。1942 年 5 月，日寇大举进犯浙赣线，周边地区纷纷告急，于是，决策层最终决定以相对偏远的云和为临时省会。时任省政府主席的黄绍竑于 1945 年在云和写了《五十回忆》一书。在书中，他曾深情地赞叹云和人民在国难当头时义无反顾的付出与牺牲。

一个感人的细节是，当时的云和因人口骤增而使得物资供应极为匮乏。1945 年春节，云和各界便自发组织起筹备会，发动民众捐得猪肉、黄酒、年糕、青菜、鸡鸭、粽子以及奎宁丸等实物，连同募款 100 多万元，对驻云部队进行了隆重的慰劳，极大地鼓舞了官兵们抗战到底的决心。

黄绍竑公馆

值得一提的是，在著名的方山岭狙击战中，勇敢的云和各界民众不顾安危，成为我抗战部队的坚强后盾，为击溃进犯的日军做出了极大的贡献。

查史料得知，1942 年 7 月底，日军二十二师团八十联队从金华窜至丽水，企图入侵浙江省政府战时驻地云和县。8 月 2 日，松阳失守。次日，进入松阳的日军向松阳与云和交界处奔袭。此役日军出动一千余人，向云和与松阳交界的方山岭一线发起进攻。进犯的日军遭到浙江保安三团的迎头痛击。

方山岭下山望排村东面二里处，有一个叫"鸡公骑坳"的山坳，海拔仅 400 余米，是云和至松阳古道的必经之处。因地势相对平缓，日军试图从此山坳突破向云和进犯。幸亏得到村民的提醒，三团官兵迅速布置好新的防线，以战壕或天然岩石为掩体顽强地用步枪、手榴弹与敌人的飞机、大炮较量。在战斗进入胶着状态时，从县城赶来的民众以及附近村民，甚至还有念着"阿弥陀佛"的僧人，纷纷赶来参与运送弹药、抢救伤员，并协助后勤部队及时送餐送水。

战斗持续了三天三夜，我抗日军民同仇敌忾，终于击退了气焰嚣张的进犯日军。

被抗战史家称为"小战役，定大局"的方山岭大捷，成功地阻止了日寇对云和的进犯，其企图摧毁临时省会，瓦解浙江军民抗战斗志的狼子野心终究没能得逞。

云和人的家国情怀也镌刻在小顺兵工厂的历史记忆里。

1938年4月，鉴于日益吃紧的战事，黄绍竑决定把从省城杭州南撤的铁工厂迁到水陆交通便利、易守难攻的小顺，专门生产前线急需的步枪、机枪、子弹、手榴弹和枪榴弹。

短短几年时间，这家名为浙江省铁工厂的兵工厂迅速发展壮大，在附近开办了3家分厂，工人从1000多人发展到4000多人，机器也从二三十台增加到一千多台。到了1942年，兵工厂每月能生产1000多支步枪、50多挺轻机枪，以及6万多颗手榴弹、枪榴弹。这些武器弹药不仅满足了浙江省的抗战需要，而且还被运往了外地，为全国的抗战立下汗马功劳。时任国民政府军事委员会政治部副部长的周恩来曾莅临兵工厂发表演说，鼓励工人"多造枪械打鬼子！"

作为浙江抗战时期最大的军工企业，小顺兵工厂的工人最多时达数千人之多。其中有多少云和籍工人自然已无法一一细考，但肯定为数不少。

1975年我在云中读初中的时候，我的同桌是新华厂的。当时作为三线军工企业，新华厂的主要产品是步枪。那个年代的他总是以自己的父母是造枪的工人而自豪。结果，隔壁班的一位同学却颇

今日小顺即景

为不屑地说:"我爷爷当初在小顺还是造机枪的呢!"包括我在内的大家自然是不信,结果还是学校里教历史的王公度老师肯定了这一史实。

其实,在一些研究丽水抗战史的专家看来,云和民众对兵工厂的更大贡献是后勤保障。据《丽水抗战口述史》一书记载,因为当时兵工厂工人的增多,住宿问题异常严峻。善良而深明大义的小顺村民,甚至把家族的祠堂腾空了用以救急。

伴随着石塘水库的建设,昔日兵工厂旧址已沉入水下。但云和民众对这座兵工厂的贡献是不会被时光所淹没的。

其实,在云和,和善之德于家国情怀中的彰显又岂止体现在抗战时期呢。

　　上世纪 60 年代，国家决定自行设计、自力更生建造新安江水电站。水电站建设需要对淳安、建德的库区民众进行大规模的移民。云和成为库区移民的一个重要迁入地。五十多年过去了，当年的移民和云和的原住民结姻缘、通习俗、共创业，成为了和睦相处的一家人。

　　记得有一次在学校的食堂用餐，无意间听到一位以前也熟悉的物理系老师用地道的云和话在与对方通话。于是，我便很兴奋地用云和话和他打招呼。原来他在考入原杭州大学物理系之前一直生活在云和。他父亲当年是淳安县排岭人，后来移民到了云和县的安溪乡，并在当地娶妻生子，成家立业。他说，他童年最美好的记忆就是作为地道云和人的母亲给他们全家炸尖削①和油筒饼②吃；最温馨的记忆则是母亲耐心地教奶奶如何做山麻糍③，如何把新鲜的香菇晒成香菇干，以及如何晒番薯条和柿子饼。

① 　作为云和的代表性小吃，尖削在云和旅游网及一些文章中被写作煎雀。我一直觉得此名不仅方言的读音不对，而且义理也不通。因为这个点心既不是油煎的，形状也不似飞雀。在一次正月里拜年时我向赤石一位长辈讨教，他告诉我应该写作尖削。它描述的是这点心两头尖尖形如刀削。我觉得甚是有理，故更其名为尖削。它以糯米、红薯和冷开水依据一定的比例搓成圆柱体下油锅炸至金黄，口感皮脆而内糯，柔软而不黏口，是云和城乡居民春节时的必备点心。

② 　油筒饼是云和的另一个代表性小吃。它以南瓜或萝卜切丝为主材，和以面粉，放置于形如油筒的铁质器皿里下油锅炸至金黄，其口感松脆爽口，回味无穷。

③ 　又称绿豆腐、观音豆腐。它以一种学名叫腐婢的灌木树叶汁为原材料，加以灰碱或石膏为凝固剂而制成，其品相晶莹剔透，可煮汤也可凉拌，不仅口感柔软清新，而且有清凉解毒之功效。

云和特产：笋干、番薯条、柿饼

斗转星移，世事轮回。1978 年开工的紧水滩水电站使得云和的大量库区移民将不得不离开生于斯长于斯的故土。

我堂哥黄加建一家就被安置在湖州一处颇为偏僻之地——妙西。在他们移民后不久的一次见面时，堂哥告诉我，这个被称为妙西的安置地，其荒凉的程度真的是大大地出乎他一家人的意料之外。但堂哥以及与他一起从赤石移民出来的乡亲们并没有抱怨，而是以十分的努力和百倍的勤劳迅速地在那里安顿下来。堂哥的大女儿在那里中专毕业后成为了当地丝织厂的技术骨干，后来还做了分管技术的副厂长；小女儿在那里考上了浙江大学，本科毕业时因成绩优异被免试推荐直读博士，成为了赤石乡有史以来的第二位博士。而且，无独有偶的是，赤石乡的第一位博士，也来自与堂哥一起移民出来的家庭。

这些紧水滩库区移民舍小家为国家的感人事迹曾经被浙江卫视的《浙江新闻联播》报道过。堂哥告诉我，那一晚看电视时他们一家人盯着屏幕的双眼无一不饱含着激动的热泪。

我想，这就是云和人的家国情怀。

泄洪中的紧水滩大坝

6. 和善之德的现代传承与弘扬光大

The Modernization and Innovation of Kindness

从悦纳一千多年前迁徙而来的畲民到善待新中国第一座自主设计并建设水电站的库区移民，从积极投身硝烟弥漫抗日战场到紧水滩水电站的外迁移民的艰苦创业，从孝子坊、百岁坊、五代同堂匾的故事到小顺兵工厂的纪念碑……云和的居民已经浇筑了无数座和善之德的历史丰碑。

重要的还在于，在云和，这一"和"文化的传统在现代不仅得以继承，而且正被不断地弘扬光大。

比如，以"帮助别人，快乐自己"为服务宗旨的"老李帮忙团"，其注册的志愿者人数已多达 4000 余人，其无偿服务的领域几乎覆盖了民生的所有领域，时至今日"老李帮忙团"已成为诠释这座和善之城的最亮丽名片。

被称为"信义孤儿"的叶石云，从十一岁那年开始用六年时间的坚持，以捡废品、打短工、省下救助款等方式还清了父母生前欠下的所有债务，书写了信义之德在今日云和的最美篇章。

被誉为"最美夜行者"的水务集团职工廖伟平，在无数个寒来暑往、夜深人静的夜晚，他手握着一条"听漏棒"行走在大街小巷，用心守护着整个县城的用水安全。

被学生称为"燕子姐姐"的云和第三中学体育老师钟华燕，自从组建了"云之梦"健美操队后，她几乎没有寒暑假、没有节假日地与孩子们在一起摸爬滚打。这群山里娃在她的带领下获奖无数，甚至还登上了《中国梦想秀》的舞台。

还比如，以"和信"为基本经营理念创造了木玩世家传奇故事的著名企业家何尚清、积极帮扶贫困学子和残疾人群体的企业经营者陈可云、放弃杭州的城市生活回乡积极为村民们谋福利的村支书金建忠、无论严寒酷暑或白天黑夜随时出现在患者身边的乡村医生陈子贵、克服人员和经费不足等困难，使云和县图书馆的古籍工作走在了全国县级图书馆前列的潘丽敏、三十年如一日悉心照顾行动不便的公公婆婆和患病小叔的普通村民蓝香梅、不顾个人安危勇救三个落水孩子的供电公司职工冯建鸿与徐东东、冒着生命危险冲进火海救出行动不便老人的农信社职工毛征伟、收留生活无法自理的流浪汉并将其视若己出的叶世海……

我相信，如果把这些和善之德的践行者一一写出来，那将是一份长长的芳名录。

如果说如上这些和善者的故事只是我从新闻报道中萃取而来的话，那么接下来的故事则是我亲历的。

故事的主人公是我的三位班主任：

我从赤石小学转学到贵溪小学时的班主任有个很雅致的名字：潘金鸾。那个时候我们的小学有个贫下中农管理委员会，简称贫管会。这是学校在那个年代里最高的权力机构。在贫管会的眼中，书本知识的学习远没有学工、学农、学军重要。但我们的潘老师却以自己师者的良知每每找机会或寻借口把我们从田野里叫回教室上课。她有一句口头禅："你们不好好上课将来要后悔的！"

记得有一次，也许是贪玩的缘故，二十多人的班级只回来寥寥几个同学，但潘老师照样异常认真地给我们几个人讲了一堂课。多年之后恢复了高考,我们这个班有三人考上了本科,尤其是我还成为了那一年应届生中的文科第一名。要知道,这可是整个云和县应届生里只有八人考上本科的 1979 年,贵溪小学仅是一所乡村小学。

我初中的班主任是魏源仙。书香门第出身的她因品学兼优而在云和中学留校任教。也许是魏老师自己太优秀了,她对学生的要求也特别严格。记得云和中学当时的负责人叫严厉,可大家在背后里说我们的班主任"魏老师比严厉还要严厉!"

但就是这样一位严厉的班主任,却因为我在运动会上跑 400 米冲刺时摔破了膝盖而心疼得直抹眼泪。反倒是我若无其事地劝她:"虽然摔了一跤,但好歹为班级争回了第一的名次。"魏老师摆了摆手决然地告诉我说,她情愿不要这个第一名!

我高一时的班主任是吴爱萍。吴老师在做班主任的同时还教我们班的语文课。那个时候已经恢复高考了。鉴于作文在高考语文卷中的重要性,语文教研组在 1978 年的国庆节前组织了一场全校作文竞赛。在不久后公布的成绩栏里,我发现自己获得了高一年级段的第一名,为此很是风光和自得了一阵子。

二十年后的一个暑期,我回母校参加同学会,在一个很偶然的场合中得知,当年语文组讨论得奖名单时对高一段的人选大家其实更倾向于推荐吴老师的女儿徐薇。可在场的吴老师却极力反对。

她的理由是她刚刚激发起我对作文的兴趣,积极性要扬而不可抑。至于自己的孩子,她说随时随地可以对其进行辅导的。见还有老师持异议时,吴老师干脆给自己女儿的作文找出了一个"没有凸显阶级性"的缺点。要知道,这个缺点在那个年代是不被宽容的。后来我找机会向徐薇求证时,她淡然一笑说:"如果她不那么做,她就不是我妈了!"

很多年之后,我应邀在杭州电视台综合频道主讲"应杭说道"的节目。记得在录制教师节播的那一期内容时,我颇为动情地讲述了上述三位班主任的故事。我的录播助理、浙江传媒学院的一位大四女孩眼眶里泛着晶莹的泪花对我说:"教授,您真幸运!"后来,栏目监制告诉我那一期节目播出后,观众反响特别热烈。

在云和,让人感动的又岂止是师者的和善呢。

1974年夏日的一个傍晚时分,顽皮的我与一帮小伙伴玩解放军捉特务的游戏,结果不慎从父亲厂里在建的食堂大楼的三楼摔下来,昏迷不醒。好不容易打通了县城医院的急救电话,却被告知医院唯一的一辆救护车外出了。

闻讯赶到的几位邻居二话不说,借来了厂里食堂买菜用的人力三轮车,一人在前蹬,两人在后侧一左一右助推,飞奔着朝县医院赶去。不省人事的我血肉模糊地躺在父亲的怀里,自然什么也不记得。后来,每次听父亲描述起那晚的动人场景时,心中总难免感慨万千。

这是这座城邻里之间的和善。

1980 年的寒假，浙南下了一场罕见的大雪。从上海返家过寒假的我必须在金华转车。未曾料想的是，我乘坐的从金华到云和的长途班车因封道而被困在了丽水车站。望着漫天飞舞一时半会估计停不下来的大雪，归家心切的我和一位在车站里结识的云和籍旅伴决定步行回家。

走了整整一天，疲倦不堪的我俩于傍晚时分走到了离县城尚有十余里地的局村乡溪口村。这位同行者的家就在这村子里，他热情地邀请我去他家歇歇脚再走。

瑞雪兆丰年

令我感动不已的是，这位同行者的父母不仅招待我吃了一顿热乎乎的农家饭，而且见我一副身心疲惫的样子，便一再邀请我住他家歇好脚，明天再走。第二天，好客的主人还给我煮了一只鸡蛋让我带在路上吃。

这是这座城对陌生人的和善。

2017年，我那不幸罹患阿尔茨海默病（即俗称的老年痴呆症）长达八年之久的父亲，在其生命的最后一段时光里，一直陷于深度的昏迷之中。

当我们兄弟俩面对重症的老父一筹莫展时，是云和中西医结

下乡途中的公务员

康养中心的幸福老人

合医院（即现在的云和城南综合医院）的邱云伟主任医生及时伸出了援手，毅然收留了我的老父亲。邱医生和他的同事以医者的仁心仁术竭尽全力减缓了老父亲临终前的病痛，使父亲在弥留之际显得特别地平静和安详。

这是这座城医者的和善。

2019 年的暑期，因为"和文化"课题调研和走访的需要，我们开着车上山下乡、东奔西走。结果在一次去龙门的路上，车意外熄火了。经过手机搜寻，我们发现附近的紧水滩镇有一家修理铺。我赶紧派人前往求救。很快就来了个年轻的修理工，只见他打开引擎盖，不一会就把车修好了。

当我们要付钱的时候，他却摆摆手说："仅仅是举手之劳的一点小问题，不好意思收钱的。"望着他骑电瓶车离去的背影，我们除了连连地说"谢谢"之外，真不知怎么表达内心的感激之情。

这是这座城经营者的和善。

行文至此，我还想特别地记录一下云和为政者的和善。

从行政学的学理表述来说，为政者的和善也即善政。作为和善之德的一道亮丽风景线，云和的为政者在善政方面的业绩一直颇受好评。这次我们课题组在调研与走访中，更是有了真真切切的感受。我们发现上至县委书记、县长下至街道书记主任、村支书村

老街与古宅

老街与新春

委会主任，他们对云和绿水青山的悉心呵护、对民生问题的着力解决、对旧城改造的良苦用心，无一不彰显出他们在坚守初心方面的殚精竭力。

比如"梯田书记"任淑女。当初她来云和主政出任县委书记时，决定以旅游业为抓手，助推云和区域经济迈上新台阶。这期间，为了云和梯田成功获批 AAAA 景区，她可谓是煞费苦心。因为一次次不厌其烦地去北京的相关部委汇报、沟通云和梯田的相关事宜，部委相关处室的人便给了她一个"梯田书记"的名号。

又比如"云和师傅之父"王新荣。上世纪九十年代起一些拥有一技之长的云和农民远赴江西、湖北等地从事食用菌种植和销售。这触发了分管领导王新荣的灵感，他开始致力于"云和师傅"项目的推广。现如今的"云和师傅"们不仅自己赚了钱，还极大地助推了当地经济的发展。"云和师傅"作为云和实施异地综合开发的"金名片"，是全省首个也是迄今为止唯一一个省级著名劳务商标和质量品牌。也因此，"云和师傅"其人其事已多次被包括央视在内的国家级媒体所报道。

还比如"玩具县长"马国华。在今天的云和，木制玩具作为其主打产业已是蜚声海内外。有媒体曾这样报道称："在云和诗意般

　　　　　　　挥汗如雨的云和师傅

的山水风光中,孕育起一个惊艳中外的木制玩具产业。"作为当时县政府的分管副县长,马国华为木制玩具业的做大做强走南闯北,可谓呕心沥血。正是因为这些付出,马国华不仅赢得了"玩具县长"的美誉,而且他还被推选为云和木制玩具协会的终身名誉会长。

再比如,"板栗书记"林少青。当初他任石塘镇党委书记时发现村民们的日子过得实在太困苦了。于是他就想,这漫山遍野如果种上了板栗既不破坏绿水青山,又能以规模效应为村民们脱贫致富找到切合实际的路径。说干就干从来是林少青的性格。他通过发动群众、招商引资、联合林业局入股等方式,仅用三年时间便实现了建万亩板栗基地的目标。

地理标志性产品: 云和雪梨和黑木耳

可以肯定地说,如果要把云和善政的积极践行者一一罗列,这也将是一份长长的名录。

说到这座和善之城的善政,有一个细节尤其值得一提:

那天在向县委叶伯军书记汇报完云和"和"文化项目的相关进展之后,我带着几位第一次来云和的研究生在颇有年代感的县府大院里转了一圈。当我们一行人离开县府大院步行回下榻的酒店时,正是华灯初上时分,县城的街景还真相当不错。这时,我们当中的一位情不自禁地感慨道:"相比于书记办公室的简陋和县府大院的老旧,云和的县城倒是有点美轮美奂的感觉!"

作为东道主的我接过这一话题,便给学生介绍起县城的由来。云和县城所在地原称箬溪镇,因溪得名。新中国成立后改称城关镇。它位居云和盆地的中心,四周有崇山峻岭环抱,自西向东有浮云溪、箬溪款款穿城而过。正是这一优越的地理环境,使其自明景泰年间起就一直是县衙所在地。

虽然有优越的地理环境,但毕竟远离大都市,县城的规模和民生状况一直颇显颓靡。记得上个世纪七十年代在云和中学读书的时候,我的地理老师朱佐成说了一段描述云和县城的民谣,我至今还清晰地记得:"一条解放街,三爿豆腐店,街头在吆喝,街尾听得见!"它把一个区域窄小、店家稀疏的旧县城描述得惟妙惟肖。

现如今的县城可谓是发生了沧海桑田般的巨变。在历届县委、县政府善政理念的引领下，在全县人民的努力下，"小县大城"的格局已大见成效。全县总人口虽只有 11.4 万，但 80% 的人口在县城居住、93.4% 的学生在县城就读、96% 的企业在县城发展，城镇化率达 69.6%。这一治理成果被学界誉为"山区城镇化"发展的新模式。更值得期待的是，在进入后"小县大城"时

代的云和，县委叶伯军书记和他的同事们眼下正积极落实市委赋予云和打造全国山区新型城镇化样板县域的新使命。

我们有理由相信，未来的云和县城一定会展露出她更智慧、更宜居、更和美的曼妙风姿。

浮云溪畔县城新貌

结束语
Conclusion

在对云和之"和"做人与自然之间的和谐、人与他人之间的和善这两个维度的文化学解读后，我们也许可以依据这样的思路提出"云水胜境、和善之城"的城市形象宣传语。"云水胜境"呈现的是人与自然的"和"；"和善之城"凸显的是人与他人（以及由许多他人构成的社会与国家）的"和"。

众所周知，中华的"和"文化历史传承极为悠久。据专家考证"和"字是最早出现的一批汉字，金文里即有辑录。重要的还在于，以和为贵的理念一直是中华传统文化的道统。这就正如习主席概括的那样：中国"和"文化源远流长，蕴涵着天人合一的宇宙观、协和万邦的国际观、和而不同的社会观、人心和善的道德观。[①]

① 习近平：在中国国际友好大会暨中国人民对外友好协会成立 60 周年纪念活动上的讲话，《人民日报》2014 年 5 月 15 日第一版。

我们以中华传统的"和"文化理论为学理依据，在人与自然的和谐、人与他人的和善两个维度上对云和之"和"进行文化学的解读，正是贯彻落实习主席关于"和"文化讲话精神的一个具体体现，是对文化自信构建在特定地域里的一个切实努力。

重要的还在于，这一研究也颇具由小见大的意蕴。这就正如云和县委宣传部副部长陈婧伊在我们课题组汇报上曾提及的那样：云和之"和"的文化研究固然只是一城一域的"小和"，但它却可以为人类命运共同体的"大和"提供一份中国样本。

有学者曾对《永乐大典》这部集中国文化之大成的旷世大典进行了大数据分析，发现此书共涉及汉字四万多个，但常用汉字约一万字左右，而"和"是这一万个常用字里出现频率最高的汉字之一，可谓万里挑一。巧合的是，云和也是个"万里挑一"的地方，它的面积是全国的万分之一，人口也是全国的万分之一。这两个"万里挑一"的巧合，让我和我的课题组成员对云和的"和"文化研究平添了几分使命感和自豪感。

我们坚信，在县委、县政府的领导下，通过全县人民的积极参与，我们新时代的云和儿女不仅可以将云和的"和"文化传承好，而且一定会在新的历史条件下将其弘扬光大，从而为云和打造全国山区新型城镇化样板县域提供重要的精神动力。

石浦花海

后记
Postscript

　　以我的感觉而言，应该没有人会质疑"和"已成为云和这座城最贴切的城市标识和文化识别码。也就是说，正如建德做"德"文章、嘉善做"善"文章，慈溪做"慈"文章那样，县委县政府提出把"和"作为云和城市文化的核心予以精心打造和培育的思路无疑是非常精当的。这不仅是因为先人留给了我们后人"云和"这一美妙的称谓，更重要的还在于，在县委、县政府的积极引领下，各部门、各乡镇、各街道在实践"和"文化方面已经做了大量可贵的实践探索。

　　据此，我认为提炼云和的城市精神、策划城市形象的相关宣传口号、设计城市标识（Logo），以及实施城市文化品牌建设均应该以"和"为切入点。这应该成为不再有争议的话题。我们要做的是如何沿着县委、县政府确立的这一思路多做一些具体的发掘、阐释、宣传或解读工作。

正是因此，我由衷地希望本书对云和"和"文化所做的个人解读，可以为这座城市美誉度的提升起到一定的助推作用。而且，我也自信这一助推作用是值得期待的。且不说文案的酝酿、采访和写作所付出的用心，仅就配图方面，海波老弟为本书提供了那么多精美的摄影图片就足以使读者赏心悦目。当然，也只有我知道，这些图片背后凝结了他多少个寒来暑往的艰辛与执着。

最后，我要特别感谢云和县委叶伯军书记以及县委宣传部林建文部长、陈婧伊副部长对课题研究的支持与指导，也要感谢课题组朱晓虹博士等全体成员在调研、走访以及查阅资料方面的辛勤付出。此外，还要感谢丽水职业技术学院的周玲俐在英文翻译过程中付出的努力。我相信这个努力对于我们把云和"和"文化的故事传播到海外会起到积极的推进作用。

是为后记。

张应杭

2020 年 1 月 28 日于云和浮云小区

Boats in the Yunhehu Lake

Part One 上篇

The word "He" in Yunhe means the harmony between man and nature.

From the perspective of culturology, this is the unity of heaven and man in the Chinese "He" Culture. In the relationship between heaven and man, unlike the western concept of conquering nature, the excellent Chinese traditional culture has always advocated to living in harmony with nature and complementing each other, which can be explained as "The world and earth live together with me, and everything is one with me". [1]

Surrounded by the clouds and waters in Yunhe, we can most truly and intuitively feel the beautiful mood of the unity of man and heaven.

——Inscription

---

[1] It's said by a Chinese philosopher — "Zhuangzi", who, together with Laozi, were representatives of Taoism. In Taoism, the theory that man and nature are united as one is the fundamental philosophical stand.

1.My Hometown:
A Wonderland of Clouds and Waters

云水胜境是故乡

In 1970, I returned to my hometown Yunhe with my father, who moved back from Hangzhou Oxygen Concentrator Factory to participate in the establishment of Yunhe Motor Factory as a technical expert. Because the factory had not yet been built, we family members, naturally have no family houses in downtown to live in. Our mother took us back to Chishi (赤石), a rural area in Yunhe where my parents grew up.

I attended Chishi Primary School and my class supervisor and Chinese teacher was Ms. Wu. Once she assigned us a writing

Life by the riverside

task with the title of "The River in My Hometown". Inspired by my mother's suggestion about for a different and creative perspective, my short essay, describing the clouds and mist that often rose above Daxi River①, was finally taken as an example by Ms. Wu.

① Daxi River is one of the mainstreams of Wenzhou River, which is the second longest river in Zhejiang. It is officially called Longquan River in Yunhe territory, but when it flows through Chishi, it is customary for locals to call it Daxi River.

Water, clouds, and the sky

Decades have passed, and the specific text of my essay has long been forgotten, but the theme is still vaguely remembered. It was something about my understanding of the clouds and mist above Daxi River: they should be caused by the rising of the river water, and then turned into rain, which finally returned to the embrace of Daxi River from all directions as drizzles. Ms. Wu read my composition aloud to the class with her slightly accented Mandarin. After reading, she gave a comment on my writing and my imagination was highly remarked.

Many years later, when I visited Ms. Wu, who had retired and lived in a downtown apartment, she still mentioned my composition, thinking fondly of the clouds and mist around Daxi River, especially the picturesque scenery where wooden boats dotted the river in an everchanging haze.

At that moment, it occurred to me that the harmonious relationship between man and nature, which is implied in the word "He" in Chinese, can be described as: Yun Shui Sheng Jing, which means — "Wonderland of Clouds and Waters".

Since then, I have always been fond of using "Yun Shui Sheng Jing" to describe my hometown Yunhe, rather than "Shan Shui Jia Yuan" [1] .Because in my mind the former is more expressive in showing the features of Yunhe's natural beauty. If we do some research on the data, we will find that Fuyun Xiang, one of the sources of the county's name "Yunhe", was originally named after Fuyun River [2]. I guess there should have been clouds and mist floating above the river. It just confirms in some degree that Yunhe has had the natural beauty of clouds and waters since ancient times.

In fact, as far as mountains and waters are concerned, there are countless famous mountains and rivers in China, and there are countless city's propaganda slogans that highlight local mountains and rivers. But there are not many mountains and rivers that has a poetic combination of clouds and waters like Yunhe's landscape. Of course, it benefited from Yunhe's special geographical latitude and hilly areas. However, it should not be ignored that generations of the local people have been taking good care of the forests, vegetation, water and soil.

[1] Shan Shui Jia Yuan is used officially to describe Yunhe for city propaganda, which means "Homeland of Mountains and Waters".

[2] When Daxi River passes by Jinshuitan Hydropower Station and flows down, it is called Fuyun River in Yunhe. "Fu" means "float", and "Yun" means "clouds" in Chinese.

One summer vacation I accompanied my aunt to Yecunping, a hillside village where the She[1] people lived. My aunt taught in the Department of Literature and History, Provincial Party School, and has always been interested in the research of the She culture. This trip made me unexpectedly see a stole tablet called"Fengxian Shijin"[2] on a wall in the village. According to the inscription, the stone monument was erected in 1854. One of the banned contents on the stele is that if someone steals and cuts pine trees, fir trees, camellia trees, tung trees, etc., not only will they be fined, but also be asked not to offend again, or they will be charged with prison. Looking at the mottled stele, I saw our ancestors' respect for nature.

What's more important is that, despite the passing of time, the people of this city have inherited this tradition of treating nature well. For example, I once saw an information record saying that in the era of iron and steel smelting[3], several village cadres and villagers in Mayang[4] Village spontaneously took turns to protect forest resources from being cut down, patrolling the mountains day and night.

---

[1] "She" (畲) is one of the 56 ethnic groups in China.

[2] It's a ban written on stones for the protection of forests in the Qing Dynasty of China.

[3] From November 1957 to December 1958, the Communist Party of China launched a nationwide steelmaking campaign.

[4] An administrative village in Chishi Township, Yunhe County.

These rustic villagers may not know Taoist philosophy, such as the proposition of the unity of heaven and man, and they may not have the leisure time to taste the poetry unique to the literati who enjoys the beautiful scenery of the clouds and waters. They did this because they knew: without vegetation, water and soil would be lost; without the nourishment of water and soil, people and all things in nature would be displaced.

Today, Yunhe, with its green development index ranking first in Zhejiang Province, has become the first National Ecological County in Lishui, and is known as "China's Natural Oxygen Bar". It is undoubtedly the achievements of the people who live on this land and treat nature kindly with hard work and persistence.

Flowers bloom in seasons

119

It is precisely because of such a historical and cultural heritage of awe and kindness to nature that Yunhe's mountains, rivers and waters show a special "affinity" with people. Yunhe has been known as "A Blessed Land" since ancient times, which, in my mind, is a vivid reflection of the affinity. Moreover, the environment in which clouds and waters coexist harmoniously undoubtedly adds beauty and poetry to this affinity.

I often think that while we are living in the good environment of clouds and waters, feeling lucky and proud, we should also inherit this cultural tradition of awe and kindness to nature.

A Lonely boat surrounded by the clouds

2.Changting Beach:
Trimming Clouds and Cutting Waters

"裁云剪水"的长汀沙滩

On the relationship between man and nature, the West has always had the argument between anthropocentrism and non-anthropocentrism. The anthropocentrism position holds that "human beings are ends". In other words, for the purpose of survival and development, human beings can use nature as a means to achieve their ends. It directly leads to the emergence of ecological crises such as air pollution, water depletion, and intensified desertification.

Therefore, in order to face and deal with the ecological crisis, non-anthropocentrism theory comes into being. This theory advocates that "nature is end", believing that human beings must protect the ecological environment at the cost of economic growth. However, those with anthropocentrism stand back and say, "Isn't protecting nature for the better survival and development of mankind? If man's survival and development are not taken into account, wouldn't that be a case of 'putting the cart before the horse'?"

The Chinese traditional principle of the unity of heaven and man can obviously provide new ideas for getting rid of the debate between the two sides. Judging from Yunhe's case, this idea can be described as: Trim clouds and cut waters, and the beauty of harmony appears.

If you do some research on the etymology, the term "trim clouds and cut waters" is from Tu Long's [1] poem, which is used to describe the subtle and novel ideas of poems. I use this term to mean human's proper use and transformation of nature. In other words, for the survival and development of human beings, it is a must for mankind to obtain necessary living materials from the natural world, which is understandable. Faced with nature and doing nothing, human beings will not be able to survive. It is

[1] A poet in the Ming Dynasty of China.

obviously unwise for Western non-anthropocentrists to ignore this basic fact.

In fact, "trimming clouds and cutting waters" is human nature. As far as Yunhe is concerned, in ancient times the ingenious technique of reclaiming mountains into terraces and the boats sailing across the mudflats are "trimming clouds and cutting waters"; the modern Jinshuitan Hydropower Station, the cage-culture in Yunhehu Lake, and the cultivation of improved black fungi and mushrooms are also "trimming clouds and cutting waters".

But the more important thing is that, as far as the relationship between man and nature is concerned, the ingenuity of "trimming clouds and cutting waters" is an exquisite and superb craftsmanship that contains man's awe to nature, thinking highly of "harmony" and regarding it as the principle of beauty. It is for this reason that we should stick to the "beauty of harmony" position after "trimming clouds and cutting waters".

Based on this idea, Yunhe's Changting Beach came into being.

Here is the introduction of Changting Beach in Yunhe's promotional video for tourism:

This is a tourist resort built under the brilliant idea of "appreciating sea in the mountains". The people here get rich thanks to the thousand-meter artificial beach, which also help the tourist resort win great popularity. This is not only a must-visit scenic spot for tourists, but also a successful example of rural revitalization.

Before the village Changting became a tourist hotspot in Yunhe, I had been there once. At that time, I accompanied my instructor Professor Zhang Tianfei to revisit the land. Mr. Zhang was from Hangzhou. He lived with his sister's family because of his father's death at an early age. At the end of 1937, his brother-in-law, who served in the provincial government, arrived in Yunhe after Hangzhou was captured by the Japanese invaders. So his childhood was spent in Yunhe during the Anti-Japanese War.

Changting in autumn

His family once lived in a Xu's family here in Changting. After retirement, Mr.Zhang had always wanted to return to Yunhe to extend his gratitude to the honest and kind landlord Xu. As a result, we had our trip to Changting. At that time, I felt that the entire Changting Village was very dilapidated.

In 2019, when I was being filmed for the World Lishuinese Conference trailer, I took the chance to visit Changting again. As soon as I got out of the car, the artificial beach built along the river, together with the tents, beach chairs and dense crowds of tourists, made me really shocked. In a moment I felt like crossing Haitang Bay in Sanya, Hainan. But the clouds surrounding the mountainside, the mist rising over the lake, and the metasequoia trees standing in the white mist, reminded me that this was not Sanya, but the once shabby Changting Village instead.

This was my first impression of visiting Changting again. It was quite amazing.

The reason why Changting Beach is particularly worthy of appreciation is that Changting people did not plunder natural resources or even break the harmony and tranquility of nature inthe process of achieving wealth. The villagers simply "trim" the scenery where the water waves are usually foggy, and "cut" a relatively open area on the uneven pebble beach, gently covering it with a layer of sand. As a result, the tidal flats where no one wanted to linger in the past were made into a wonderful place to appreciate the "sea" in the cloudy mountains. It is a modern masterpiece of "trimming clouds and cutting waters".

I remember the poet Haizi once wrote a famous poem: I have a house, towards the sea, with spring flowers blossoming. It describes the happy life he understands. Inadvertently, Changting people have already had such an enviable life.

That day, after completing all the shooting tasks of Changting Beach, our team was reluctant to leave for a long time.

Fog rises from Wenzhou River

3.Yunhe Terraces with Clouds and Waters Adding Radiance to Each Other

云水相映的云和梯田

Compared with Changting Beach, Yunhe Terraces is obviously a more representative scenic spot for tourists. I have a friend who works at Hangzhou Normal University. When he was invited to give lectures in Lishui College, he hoped to visit Yunhe after class[①]. But he had only half a day's free time, so he asked me to recommend a place most worthwhile to visit. Without any hesitation, I recommended Yunhe Terraces, telling him that in Yunhe, the harmony between man and nature was most elegantly and perfectly displayed in these terraced fields.

① Yunhe is only 1 hour's drive from Lishui.

Indeed, Yunhe Terraces, which has been rated as one of the "Forty Beautiful Spots of China" by authoritative foreign tourism and photography publications, accompanied by seas of clouds, bamboo forests, streams, waterfalls, fog and quaint villages, depicts a most beautiful picture where human and nature are in a harmonious symbiosis. What's more, this beautiful scenery, in the chorus with nature, varies from season to season, which is really breathtaking.

If the tourists who come to Yunhe Terraces happen to meet the annual Plowing Festival, then he will be enchanted by "the most beautiful terraced fields in China" [1] , and he will surely be fascinated by the ancient wisdom underneath the harmonious relationship between man and nature. What made me a little embarrassed, however, was that my friend complained to me on the phone that Yunhe Terraces in his eyes were bland. From his point of view, in terms of area, Yunhe Terraces can't be compared to Yuanyang Terraces [2] , because the latter's variously shaped terraces are continuous, each of which covers an area of thousands of acres; in terms of the diversity of colors, Yunhe

---

[1] It's the official propaganda slogan for Yunhe Terraces.
[2] Yunyang Terraces is located in Yunnan Province, China.

Terraces is overshadowed when confronted with Jiangling Terraces [1] , where the yellow rapeseeds, distant mountains, the field's waters, white walls and misty-grey roofs form a beautiful picture. At the end of the call he asked me a question, "What on earth is the beauty of Yunhe Terraces?"

What is the beauty of this "most beautiful terraced field in China"? Bearing this question in mind, I asked Liu Haibo, a photojournalist at Yunhe Converging Media Center and member of the Chinese Photographers Association. The experienced journalist, who had taken countless terrace pictures, revealed the mystery: the unique beauty of Yunhe Terraces lies in its exquisite picture in which the clouds and waters enhance each other's beauty. It is especially amazing that this exquisite natural painting is changing every moment with its dazzling colors.

Seeing the blank expression on my face, Liu Haibo kindly invited me to experience it with him personally. I accepted the invitation with great pleasure. We agreed to meet at the viewing platform of the terraces at 5:00 the next morning.

[1] Jiangling Terraces is located in Jiangxi Province, China.

Sunrise at Yunhe Terraces

Although together with my friends, colleagues, and foreign students I had visited this landscape of my hometown countless times, I had to admit that only this time allowed me to truly appreciate the unique and beautiful scenery of Yunhe Terraces.

That day, when we met on the highest viewing platform of the terraces, there was a thick fog surrounding it, and the visibility was about ten meters. While I was worrying that the dense fog would affect our appreciation of the terraced fields, a glow of the rising sun appeared from the clouds in the distance. In the glow of light, the thick fog which seemed as if it could never be turned off just now, became a graceful veil, floating away by my side. Looking down, the layers of water-filled terraces were like mirrors, reflecting the radiance of the rays of light that had been refracted among the clouds.

With the gradually brightening light, the fog floated continuously and rose into clouds of mist. After a while, these white misty elves, from near to far, bottom to top, drifted to the distant villages, which, together with the smoke curling up from kitchen chimneys, created a poetic and lively painting in which all kinds of "clouds" met.

The concept of "Wonderland of Clouds and Waters" got the most beautiful display and interpretation at that moment.

To my surprise, at noon, the scenery of clouds and waters on the terraced fields got very different from that in the morning. If the tone of the water-filled terraces upon which the clouds were projected is reddish-brown in the morning, and then at noon the mirror-like terraces that reflected the white clouds inlaid in the blue sky were dazzling snow white, pure and with no trace of mottles. At dusk, what the countless pieces of water mirror reflected were golden clouds, noble and full.

My whole day was immersed in the beautiful clouds and waters. For a moment, I felt that all the poems and verses about clouds and waters that I had read before seemed to have become a wonderful annotation of the fascinating environment created by Yunhe Terraces.

According to Liu Haibo, the scenery created by clouds and waters in Yunhe Terraces does not only change in a single day, but also shows different kinds of beauty in spring, summer, autumn and winter. However, these different views share a wonderful commonality: when you look at the clouds, the water is under the clouds; when you look at the water, the clouds are in the water. Involved in Yunhe Terraces, you can definitely forget the troubles caused by fame and wealth in this secular world, and your heart fly freely in the clear and transparent wonderland of clouds and waters.

I believe this is probably the magic of nature to humans. This is why today's people are becoming more and more enthusiastic about escaping from the reinforced concrete cities to embrace nature.

The return to nature is the return to beauty.

Yunhe Terraces in four seasons

137

4.Where There Are Rivers[①] and Clouds, There Is Beauty in Yunhe

"十里云河" 皆美景

I remember when I went to Shanghai to register as a freshman of East China Normal University in 1979, I introduced my hometown Yunhe to my senior schoolmate, who was responsible for picking up freshmen at the train station. After my introduction, the warm-hearted senior replied, "I know that Teresa Teng has a song called *Yunhe*. It turns out there is really such a place!"[②]

① There are many streams of rivers in Yunhe that converge in different places, which together with other mainstreams create the well-known Wenzhou River.

② The place name Yunhe (云和) and the song Yunhe (云河) share the same pronunciation. The latter can be explained as "River of Clouds" or "Clouds and Rivers", which, firstly pointed out by the senior schoolmate due to misunderstanding, shed insight into the writer's perception of his hometown later on.

Many years later, when I saw the term "Shili Yunhe" (十 里 云 河) [1] on the website promoting Yunhe for tourism, all of a sudden I recalled my senior's anecdote in 1979. It is said that the creative idea of "Shili Yunhe" comes from Yunhe's cultural celebrity Chen Huimin. Mr.Chen, a talented Peking University student, was assigned to Yunhe's countryside to teach because of historical reasons [2], which in his eyes, however, was a "beautiful mistake". That is because Mr.Chen has regarded Yunhe as his second hometown ever since, and after years of researching local culture as his mission, he has made outstanding contributions to Yunhe's cultural and educational cause, which helps him win the respect of Yunhe people. Mr. Chen has had many honorary titles, among which the most recent one was obtained during the World Lishuinese Conference in 2019, where he was named "the Cover Person of Yunhe".

I think Mr. Chen's idea of "Shili Yunhe" is extraordinarily subtle and ingenious. Just by a few words, the term accurately and romantically depicts the unique scenery of the eight-hundred-mile Wenzhou River in Yunhe.

---

[1] "Shili Yunhe" (十里云河) contains two meanings: "river of clouds that extends for some 5 kilometers" and "clouds and rivers that stretch for some 5 kilometers".

[2] From the 1950s to the late 1970s, due to political reasons, a large number of urban educated youths in China left cities to settle in rural areas and took part in the labor force there.

The Wenzhou River in Yunhe territory, starting from the Yunhehu [1] Lake formed by the dam of Jinshuitan Hydropower Station, winds ten miles to the border of Liandu district, Lishui city. The river is dotted with scenic spots such as Huiyun Temple, Shipu Flower Sea, Changting Beach, Fanying Xiaoshun, and Shuimo Guixi. These scenic spots come along the beautiful Wenzhou River, and continuously present artistic pictures of the beautiful cloud-water scenery.

Of all the scenic spots mentioned above, Yunhehu Lake is undoubtedly the most recommended place. Seen from the distance, the little sailboats scattered on the mirror-like surface of the lake, the quaint village houses, the snow pear blossoms blooming on the banks and the contented waterfowls, evoke Yunhenese childhood memories of the local boat culture.

---

[1] Yunhehu(云和湖) Lake, the second largest artificial lake in Zhejiang Province, is located in the northern part of Yunhe County. With more than 50 square kilometers' water coverage, the lake's total storage capacity is 1.4 billion cubic meters.

Yunhehu Lake

Personally, I have a stronger connection with Yunhehu Lake. That is because the quiet land's downstream is the place where I was born and raised—Chishi. It is a typical ancient town built near the river in Southern China. In the old days when transportations largely depended on waterways, Chishi used to have a large population with numerous businessmen and vendors crowding the streets. There were as many as eight docks, on the both sides of which lined up wooden houses built on stilts. In my childhood memory, every summer night, I used to hunch over the balcony of those wooden houses, watching the ships come and go, or listening to adults telling stories from *Romance of the Three Kingdoms* and *Water Margin*, which was really enjoyable to me as a kid.

Later, due to the construction of the Jinshuitan Hydropower Station, this ancient town ceased to exist on June 24, 1986. On this day, the dam began to store water. Since then, the ancient town of Chishi has become an indelible memory of our nostalgia.

One summer vacation, I took my international students to Yunhehu Lake for a visit. During the trip, I told them about my childhood memories that had "sunk" under the lake. I found an American boy named Mark turn a deaf ear to me, staring at the mountains on the shore. Later, after a close chat with him, I learned that he was attracted by the clusters of clouds on the mid-mountainside after the rain. The student, who grew up in the New York metropolis, has never seen clouds so close. He asked me where these clouds came from. I told him that the condensed water vapor from the vegetation and the mist rising from the lake were the answers. After a moment, he was very excited to tell me that he finally knew why Yunhehu Lake had got the name! He told me that "he"(和)should mean "and". In other words, "Yunhehu (云和湖) Lake" should be "clouds and lakes".[1] He said

① This is a new explanation given by Mark, who got inspiration from the mid-mountainside clouds. In Chinese, while "Yun" (云) means clouds and "Hu" (湖) means lakes, the word "He"(和) has both the meaning of "Harmony" and "And". Mark chose the latter explanation, while most people just regard "Yunhehu" (云和湖) as place names.

Shadow of the departing sails

Between clouds and water

he would strongly advise that the propaganda words should convey this message to tourists: it's a beautiful story from nature about how the clouds and lakes coexist harmoniously.

I was stunned by Mark's Chinese proficiency and imagination. Later, when I had a chance to meet a friend who worked in Yunhe Culture and Tourism Bureau, I seriously told Mark's findings to him, believing the explanation should and can be a highlight of Yunhehu Lake for tourism. Because this story of clouds and lakes not only fits the literal meaning of "Yunhehu", but also gives Yunhehu Lake a unique characteristic that is different from the West Lake, Dongting Lake, and Jingbo Lake.

What's more important is that this unique characteristic is the essence of the word "Yunhe" (云河) which is the key word of "Shili Yunhe" (十里云河). In fact, apart from Yunhehu Lake, the main attractions along the rivers in Yunhe are all traditional Chinese ink paintings drawn by clouds and lakes. Other attractions such as the Huiyun Temple surrounded by lakes and mountains, the Changting Beach that "trims clouds and waters", the Xiaoshun village surrounded by clouds and lakes and the boat-berthing place Guixi, all have a beautiful connection with the word "Yunhe" (clouds and rivers). I think this should be why I insist on using "Yun Shui Sheng Jing" (Wonderland of Clouds and Waters) to summarize Yunhe's tourist resources.

Interestingly, this good environment of clouds and waters is also beneficial to business. On the Yunhehu Lake there is a hotel named Yunman. Yunman Hotel（云曼酒店）was called "the Maldives Hotel in Yunhe" by some travel websites and tourists. I always feel that such an expensive hotel should not have too many customers. However, once an EMBA student of mine wanted to book a room in Yunman Hotel and was told that no room was available. He finally turned me for help. After some probing, I was sorry to tell him that I could not help, because the hotel was really full that night, which really shocked me.

Later, I met the hotel's investor Huang Qiaoling at a fellowship activity in Hangzhou, and I consulted him about my confusion. As a investor, he proudly told me that the high price of his hotel lied in the unique scenery of the lakes and mountains. I was still puzzled and asked, "Aren't there lots of lakes and mountains in many other hotels?" He replied, "The views seen from Yunman Hotel not only have mountains and waters, but even more wonderfully, there are clouds and mist rising from the lake from time to time, just like a fairy garden." I was suddenly enlightened.

Yunqi cabin

It's true that modern people, tired of living in the cities, would probably be touched by the enchanting picture where the clouds and lakes create a poetic scene. This may be the most attractive part of Yunman Hotel.

However, compared to the somewhat high-profile Yunman Hotel built in the middle of the lake, I prefer the Yunqi Wooden Houses (云栖木屋) that stand quietly on the lakeside hill. Each of the twelve independent wooden houses is not only surrounded by flowers and jungles, but also faces the Yunhehu Lake, which provides people with a panoramic view of the lake. As a result, the flowers nearby and the lake and mountains in the distance create a modern version of "retreat paradise". The founder of these wooden houses is my little fellow-Lian Qiaozhong, a young entrepreneur with a remarkable performance in Yunhe's wooden toy industry. With gratitude for his hometown, he built these wooden cabins as a B&B in Chishi in 2015, which has now become an "internet celebrity".

What impresses me particularly is that Lian named the wooden houses "Yunqi" (云栖) [1], which is very accurate. Just imagine that the clouds are rising slowly from the Yunhehu Lake, surrounding the

[1] In Chinese, "Yun" (云) means "Clouds" and "Qi" (栖) means "Stay".

wooden houses and even drifting into your window, lingering beside you, and then the natural beauty of clouds and waters has transformed into the aesthetic of life.

How wonderful and poetic the life is!

Yunhehu Lake

5.The Wonderful Sea of Clouds at Baihejian Mountain Peak [①]

白鹤尖的云海奇观

In the summer of 2019, in order to better publicize the good mountains and waters of Yunhe during the World Lishuinese Conference, I was invited by the county's United Front Work Department [②] to serve as the image ambassador in the promotional video. The film was coordinated by Chen Weifei, the deputy director of Yunhe's TV station. During the filming period,

---

① Baihejian (白鹤尖), located in the scenic area of Yunhe Terraces, is the highest mountain peak in Yunhe County.

② The United Front Work Department of CPC in China takes the lead in coordinating the work of the democratic parties, the work of non-party intellectuals, the work of non-public-owned economies' personnel, the work relating to ethnic minorities, religions, and the work concerning with Hong Kong, Macao and Taiwan.

Sea of clouds at Baihejian

I asked her how to interpret the natural scenery of Yunhe from the perspective of clouds and waters and what the most representative places of "Yun Shui Sheng Jing" were. She listed Yunhe Terraces, Yunhehu Lake, Changting Beach, but Baihejian Mountain Peak was especially recommended. Chen Weifei told me that it was an extremely beautiful place that could really compared to a fairyland.

With the expectation of the fairyland's beauty, our research group drove to Baihejian. Because we had done some previous work, we knew that Baihejian, with an elevation of 1593 meters, is the highest peak in Yunhe, and that it is known as the Four Great Mountains with Niutoushan (1297m), Lingjishan (1249m) and Lujiaojian (1166m). Baihejian Mountain Peak was so named because the peak is like a white crane and the rocks on the mountain are all white [1]. As a native Yunhenese, although I had heard of its name constantly, I had never been there. However, I had some doubts about the wonders of the sea of clouds described by Chen Weifei as a fairyland. I have been teaching for more than 30 years, and because of my natural preferences and the convenience of teaching around the world, I have experienced too many wonders of "sea of clouds". For example, the Mount Huangshan with the sea of clouds as its main viewing feature. I even had had the experience of visiting Huangshan five times, which made me believe that "A trip to Huangshan ends your interest in other seas of clouds" [2].

---

[1] Baihejian in Chinese means "White Crane Peak".

[2] It's the writer's adaptation of the famous saying in China: A trip to Huangshan ends your interest in other mountains, which denotes that the Mount Huangshan overshadows all the other mountains in China.

With my little doubt, I lay down early in the tent. Because the next morning, everyone was expected to wait for or witness the magnificent moment of sunrise in the sea of clouds. Our team was obviously looking forward to this beautiful encounter.

To everyone's surprise, we met the beauty of Baihejian's sea of clouds in advance.

Early in the morning, when there was still some time before the sunrise moment that we had been informed of previously, everyone got out of the tent with great expectation. The wind was a little bit heavy. Around the surrounding area were windmill generators scattering along with the rolling hills. These wind-driven generators glittered in silver-white in the morning sunlight, which not only enriched the white tone of Baihejian Mountain Peak, but also brought a strong modern air to the surrounding sceneries.

Suddenly, thick and moist clouds, like white elves, wrapped in the fragrance of Masson pine and wild rhododendron, rushed towards us. It seemed as if we could "drag" the clouds into our arms just with a single wave. In our exclamation,the clouds quickly dissipated with the wind, which even made us suspect that the scene surrounded by clouds and fog was unreal. But hardly had we found out whether we were in the real or the illusory world when these white elves came rushing towards us again. For a while, the clouds came and went like this, which was overwhelming. In this way, on this early morning, our encounter with the beautiful sea of clouds had begun, which seemed magical and everlasting.

Trees and clouds

It was particularly worth sharing that I found we could not only appreciate Baihejian's clouds through the eyes but also through the ears. Maybe it was because I stood very close to the clouds that a gentle sound would come into my ears as long as I listened attentively. It was really a wonderful sound of nature. I even thought that after going down the mountain, I should go to the relevant department to suggest that a pavilion be built here, which can be named "Ting Yun Xuan".[1]

Soon, staying in the fairyland of clouds, we finally met the magnificent sunrise. Unlike the sunrise of Mount Huangshan, the sunrise here came in the endless "waterfall" of clouds. The endless, waterfall-like sea of clouds was first dyed red by the rising sun, then slowly orange-yellow, and finally golden-yellow, shining with the Buddha-like beauty. No wonder some netizen left a message on the relevant website saying, "You don't have to go to Huangshan to see the sea of clouds, nor is it necessary to go to Mount Emei to see the Buddha's light, because they both exist in Baihejian Mountain Peak!" It is true.

---

[1] Ting Yun Xuan (听云轩) is a poetic name in the Chinese context. In Chinese, the character "Ting" (听) menas "Listen", "Yun" (云) means "Clouds" and "Xuan" (轩) means "Pavilion".

After admiring the magnificent sunrise adorned by the endless cloud sea, we began to wander carefreely. Someone in our group found a small temple built of stones on the mountain top. There were joss sticks[①], candles and other offerings around the temple. According to the driver who was also our tour guide, the small temple is built for the Eight Immortals. Whenever there is a drought, the villagers around will come here to ask for rain. Some of us searched the Internet immediately and found out that this little temple had quite a long history. According to the *Yunhe Chronicle* compiled during the Tongzhi period of the Qing Dynasty (1862—1875 A.D.): "Baihejian Mountain Peak is 35 miles west of the county, and it was called 'Meijiujian' by folks. It is the highest peak in the west of the county. There is a well spring where the praying for rain can be answered."

Stories about blessings or the divine manifestations of gods cannot be trusted. However, from my point of view, in a place where fogs are so abundant and the sea of clouds is so spectacular, the probability of raining will naturally be very high.

---

① Joss sticks are slender sticks of incense burned before a joss by the Chinese.

I remember the lyrics of a popular song before: There is a cloud made of rain in the wind. From the perspective of meteorology, the cloud is made of rain, and rain is in the form of cloud in the sky. When the cloud falls down, it becomes rain. It is my understanding of why our ancestors' praying for rain can be answered. While some of us applauded my explanation, some took it with a pinch of salt.

On the way back to the city, my teammates were a little tired and fell asleep. I was afraid the driver would be affected, so in order to refresh him I chatted with him. To my surprise, the young driver actually knew the song *A Cloud Made of Rain in the Wind* and knew that the singer was Meng Tingwei [1] . He told me that this song was his mother's favorite, and he was naturally familiar with it by his mother's influence. We both hummed the song gently, "*There is a cloud made of rain in the wind, a cloud made of rain; the heart of the cloud is all rain, and all the drops are you ...*"

Suddenly it occurred to me that the lyrics of this song fitted quite well with Baihejian's clouds, rains and winds. I couldn't help sighing, things in the world are sometimes so wonderful.

---

[1] Meng Tingwei (formerly known as Chen Xiumei), was born on December 22, 1969 in Taiwan, China. *A Cloud Made of Rain in the Wind* was Meng's repertoire at CCTV's Spring Festival Gala in 1995.

Clouds as waterfall

6.The Start of Clouds and Waters—Xiadongtian

云水发端处——夏洞天

Yunhe's beautiful scenery is not only in its terraces, the rivers, Yunman Hotel, Yunqi Wooden Houses or Baihejian. On the border between Yunhe County and Longquan County, there is also such a beautiful scenery of clouds and waters-Xiadongtian. This is a spot often overlooked by tourists.

There is also a beautiful legend about Xiadongtian. According to the records in *Yunhe Chronicle*, there was a woman with the surname of Liu, and when she was washing clothes by the stream, she swallowed a dragon egg accidentally due to curiosity. Three years later she gave birth to a dragon. The dragon grew up gradually and one day he carried his mother and flew to a deep pond in Chishi's Mayang Village, where they became immortals. Since then, the surprised villagers called the pond Liugu Pond [1], and the place Xianren Cave [2]. Later, the villagers also raised funds to build the Dragon Mother Palace there. This is the origin of Xiadongtian. According to historical records, the proverb "A true dragon comes from Yunhe, and the dragon's mother stays in Chishi" began to spread among folks during the Tongzhi period of the Qing Dynasty (1862-1874 A.D.).

Myths are myths after all, and they are not true of course. In the summer of 1992, when I was the Deputy Dean of the School of Humanities in Zhejiang University , I organized a trip to Yunhe for the faculty members, because the work I was in charge of included the Labor Union's travel welfare. When we traveled to Xiadongtian and talked about the legend of the Dragon Mother, a teacher of theChinese Department who studied folk myths explained that many of the legends about the dragons flying in the clouds and the wind

[1] The Liugu Pond is named after the dragon's mother, who had the surname of "Liu", and Liugu Pond means "The Pond of Ms. Liu".

[2] The place where the dragon and his mother became immortals looks like a big cave with sunshine and water pouring in from the sky, so the place was named after the dragon's story and means "The Cave of Immortals".

calling for rain often came from those places on the banks of rivers or lakes, which proved that the myth had the element of real life. Based on this, he believed it would be abnormal if there was no legend about dragons in Yunhe, a good place with clouds and waters.

That day, the teachers who had been used to sitting in a tight position were very different from usual. Everyone was playing in Liugu Pond, cooking at the side of the Dragon Mother's Palace, and making Longjing tea brought from Hangzhou with the clear spring water there. It was a very happy, comfortable and joyful day.

I remember that on the way back from Xiadongtian, it was the sunset moment when the sky was full of the evening glow, and the red clouds were reflected in the paddy water fields, which enhanced its beauty with the distant rays of smoke in the villages.

In the summer of 2019, due to the research needs of the topic of Yunhe's "He"Culture, I took some graduate students to Xiadongtian again. After the encounter with a sudden heavy rain, we found that the recurring sunlight penetrated the dense jungle and projected into the clear water of Liugu Pond. The water surface was gently flowing because of the waterfall's pouring, which was really beautiful.

More importantly, an idea flashed in my mind, which helped me find the source of the good environment of clouds and waters in Yunhe: the continuous mist in the pond, rising and floating in the jungle as clouds, then surrounds the mountain tops, and that's where the scene of "clouds" begins; the clear water of the pond, even in the dry seasons, continuously flows out of the valley, forming a stream that runs into the Wenzhou River, and that's where the scene of "waters" begins.

It was also from this that I suddenly understood why Wang Wei [1] had the verse of "Leisurely stroll to where the water ends, sit and appreciate how the clouds rise".Later generations used to interpret it as a life without fear of hopeless situation, because as long as one has a good attitude, he will finally get out and there will be a good time for appreciating clouds and rainbows. I think this verse may be a natural depiction of clouds and waters when the poet lingers in a beautiful scenery. Using these two poems to describe the waters and clouds of Xiadongtian can't be more appropriate.

---

① Wang Wei, a famous poet and painter of the Tang Dynasty in China.

Stay in the countryside

Early morning mist

When we wistfully left Xiadongtian with reluctance, there was a bit of regret of not being able to describe the beautiful scenery wholly. Since the beauty was beyond our words, the poems of the ancients may be used to respond to the situation. After I recited "*Leisurely stroll to where the water ends, sit and appreciate how the clouds rise*", Dr. Zhu Xiaohong of our research group also chanted a verse, "*The wind brings the sound of springs to the valley mouth, shadows of clouds and mountains fall into my heart*". [1] The verse quoted by Dr. Zhu to describe the beauty of Xiadongtian at that moment won everyone's admiration.

[1] It's two lines of verse in the poem "Shanjushi" (Poems about Living in the Mountains) written by Shiyanshou, a monk in the period of Five Dynasties and Ten Kingdoms (907—960 A.D.).

Indeed, for Yunhe's good environment of waters and clouds, I often regret that I don't have the reputation and talent of Su Dongpo. If I had them, I would use verses like "*The West Lake looks like a fair lady at her best, whether she is richly adorned or plainly dressed.*"[1] to make Yunhe's clouds and waters famous. If I had the spirit and calligraphy skills like Mi Fu[2], I will imitate his writing on Mount Wudang: "the Greatest Mountain"[3], and look for a boulder at Yunhehu Lake or at Yunhe's motorway exit, writing down the words "the Greatest Land of Clouds and Waters".

I even guess that the characteristic of "Lingfan"[4] in Yunhenese, which is admired by others, may be rendered by Yunhe's clouds and waters.

---

[1] It's the famous two lines of verse in Su Dongpo's poem "Poetry on the Lake After the First Clear Rain", which is well-known for the vivid description of the West Lake.

[2] A famous calligrapher, painter, calligraphy and painting theorist of the Northern Song Dynasty (960—1127 A.D.).

[3] There are many magnificent mountains well-known both at home and abroad in China. But there has been a lot of ambiguity over which mountain is "the Greatest Mountain". Mount Taishan, Mount Wudang, Mount Huangshan, and Mount Huashan are all in some people's consideration.

[4] "Lingfan" (灵范) is a commendatory word used in Yunhe's dialect to describe people who are smart and sensible.

The fishing girl

Part Two　下篇

The word"He"in Yunhe also represents the kindness between people.

Interpreted from the perspective of culturology, this is the unity of individuals which is valued in the Chinese "He" Culture. In the relationship between the individual and the society, unlike the egoistic ideas in the West and the curse of "hell is other people" (Sartre), the excellent Chinese traditional culture has always advocated living in harmony with others, which can be illustrated in the adage that "*The morally noble man brings the virtues of others to completion; he does not bring their evils to completion.*"(Confucius).

Yunhe's local culture is the most iconic and direct display of the harmonious relationship between the individual and the society.

——Inscription

1.The Kind and Inclusive Yunhe People

和善包容的云和人性格

The unique features of a local environment always give special characteristics to its inhabitants.

I remember at the end of 2002, when one of my students, who worked in the government of Yunhe at the time, talked about the characteristics of Yunhe people. He mentioned an interesting thing. As a non-native who could not speak Yunhe dialect, he was worried that he would be cheated when going to the wet market. Therefore, the young man with a high education background stood by first, watching the trade between the stall owner and other buyers, and then came forward to buy the same goods that the stall owner had just sold. To his surprise, the owner didn't raise prices, and even kindly gave him a handful of green onions for fear that the young man had insufficient seasonings.

This student urther told me that according to his observation, the Yunhenese friendly and inclusive character was not only revealed in the wet markets' hawkers and rickshaw drivers, but was also displayed in the meeting with neighbors and the friendly salutation "have you dined yet" spoken in Yunhe dialect. In addition, the character became even more obvious in the harmonious relationship between colleagues and in the kindness of leaders to subordinates, teachers to students, doctors to patients, government officials to the folks, natives to non-natives, and so on.

I asked him, "Then why do you think Yunhe people has this kind of character?" He replied, "Is it because of the natural environment of the peaceful mountains, clouds and waters? After all, there is an old saying that 'badlands beget cunning people', and so 'goodlands cultivate kind people'."

It makes some sense to explain Yunhe people's friendliness and inclusiveness from the perspective of geography. But it is still not enough. Why is it Yunhe people who form this open and kind

Writing spring couplets,

sending blessings

temperament while there are so many other similar places along the beautiful Wenzhou River? We may more likely to find the answer from the angle of culturology.

As is known to all, in the nine counties (districts) of Lishui City, Yunhe is the only one with the most migrants. Due to the multicultural habits of residents, cities of migrants are usually characterized with kindness and inclusiveness. According to historical records, there were massive migrants such as the She people, the Tingzhou people and Xin'anjiang people who had moved to Yunhe three times.

The She people migrated to Yunhe more than 1,000 years ago. Their former residence was Fenghuang Mountain in Chaozhou, Guangdong Province. According to historical records, since the Yongtai Period of the Tang Dynasty (765—766 A.D.), the She people successively moved to the county of Yunhe and Jingning. When they came here somewhat apprehensively, they were surprised to find that the local people enthusiastically call them "Shekeren"-guests from the She family! It is for this reason that a very kind vocabulary was added to Yunhe's dialect [1] .

_____

① I don't know when and where the word "Shekeren" in the dialect was mistaken for an offensive term that refers to the She people. From the perspective of semantics, I'm sure that it is definitely a popular misunderstanding.

If the She people had their own written language, I believe that they would definitely use the most beautiful vocabulary to describe how they were touched when they first arrived in Yunhe.

More than 300 years ago, the Tingzhou people in Fujian Province, who spoke Hokkien and had Fujian custom, also came to Yunhe. They were accepted by the Yunhenese, living in harmony with the native people. With their own hard work and wisdom, the Tingzhou people settled down on this land of southwestern Zhejiang and finally achieved great success. Interestingly, although it is known that Tingzhou is the birthplace of Hakkas, but unlike Tingzhou people who have moved to other places are called "Hakkas", which means "guests", they are called "the Tingzhou people" in Yunhe, and the migrants themselves are happy to accept the appellation. This phenomenon once made some experts who specialized in Hakka Culture really puzzled.

Indeed, the answer is very simple. Because there had been "guests" (the She people) in Yunhe before the Tingzhou people came to live and work on this land. Therefore, in order to distinguish from the previous "guests", they prefer to call themselves "the Tingzhou people". This detail is a vivid annotation of the migration history of Yunhe.

In the 1950s, in order to build the first Chinese-designed hydropower station-the Xin'anjiang Hydropower Station, about 300,000 residents in Xin'anjiang needed to be resettled, which was a great social project for China at that time.

In January 2009, the People's Literature Publishing House published a book entitled *National Special Action: Xin'anjiang Migrants: A Report Fifty Years Late*. The author is a descendant of migrants from the Xin'anjiang reservoir areas.

Some media commented, "A painful past submerged on the bottom of the beautiful Qiandao Lake finally surfaced." In the book, after the author faithfully restores the bitter memories of some migrants such as the poor resettlement house they received, the progressively intensified conflicts they encountered with the natives, and the resettlement fees which seemed never to arrive, he summarizes this period of history with the phrase " a tragic and heroic migration of 300,000 people in western Zhejiang." When I closed the book, I felt quite sad.

When I was studying in Yunhe High School, one of my friends was a Xin'anjiang migrant. When I went back to my hometown in the Spring Festival in 2010, I talked to him about the book. Quite interested in the research of this period of history, he admitted that the migrants who were resettled in Yunhe were lucky because his family had never experienced the bitterness mentioned in the book. His father even had married a local girl who was thought to be one of the "five golden flowers"[①] by the villagers. Moreover, as far as he knew, almost none of the Xin'anjiang migrants in Yunhe had been troubled by the problems described in the book. On the contrary, because of the kindness of the indigenous people, they soon got accustomed to the land and became new Yunhenese.

What's more, in the city of Yunhe, kindness and openness does not only exist in the relationship between the natives and migrants.

In 2012, a love story that took place in Meizhu Village in Yunhe Terraces was once made into a micro-film and was widely acclaimed. The heroine was a teacher in a university in Shanghai, who came to visit Yunhe Terraces. In a short five-day tour, she met her Mr. Right there, leaving her body and heart settled in Yunhe. As she said frankly to the media, "love the beauty of Yunhe, but love the simplicity, spirituality, and kindness of Yunhe people more." Now, *Five Days on the Clouds*, the B&B run by the hero and heroine in the love story, has become very popular on the Internet. Many tourists from all over the country came here not only for the terraces but also for the romantic love.

---

① "Golden flowers" often refers to beautiful women in Chinese.

Young girl in an ancient house

In 2013, Professor Wan Bin, a doctoral supervisor and the dean of Zhejiang Academy of Social Sciences, was invited to lecture in Lishui. After completing the lecturing task, he went to Meiwan Village in Yunhe to do a special investigation because of the needs for Zhejiang Red Culture research. But just when they were about to return, the driver found that the car could not start. It made the professor very anxious, because he must rush back to Hangzhou due to an important meeting the next day. Seeing his anxiety, a young man passing by volunteered to drive the professor to Lishui Railway Station by his own private car. The young man, who came to Meiwan to participate in the activities of the CPC, had never met the professor before.

In 2018, a story from a well-known tourism website also had a high click-through rate. The author is Mr. Lu, a tourist from Wenzhou who came to visit Yunhe by car. Because his car was broken on the way, it was in the middle of the night when he finally arrived. The shops on the streets were already closed. Unbearably hungry, he called the hotel owner for help with a try. Within 15 minutes, a few bowls of Yunhe specialty-noodles with bamboo shoots and eggs, were delivered to him and his family. The owner told him that he had already fallen asleep, but thinking of the hunger and unbearable sleeplessness he once experienced, he started to make noodles for them. Mr. Lu later said in the Moments of Wechat that the most delicious noodles he had ever tasted was in Yunhe because that bowl of noodles was seasoned with love.

In Yunhe, such stories happen almost daily. If we enter the keyword "good guys in Yunhe" in the search engine, links related to those touching stories will pop up immediately.

I think this is a natural manifestation of the kindness and inclusiveness within Yunhe people.

2.The Ubiquitous Goddess Worship

无处不在的"女神"崇拜

If "Yun Shui Sheng Jing" (Wonderland of Clouds and Waters) is a natural scenery everywhere in Yunhe, then the ubiquitous worship of "goddess" makes a cultural scenery with local characteristics. And this cultural landscape presents a spirit of kindness and friendliness.

Chen Huimin, who has studied Yunhe's regional culture, says that in the villages of Yunhe there are various goddess temples in different shapes that attract a constant stream of people.

Among these various "goddess" worships, the worship of Goddess of Heaven (Mazu) is undoubtedly best known to the public.

According to historical documents from the Song Dynasty, Mazu was originally a woman named Lin Mo on the coast of Meizhou island, Putian, Fujian Province. Because she did not cry at birth, her father named her "Mo"[1]. Once, a merchant ship was struck by a gale while passing by Meizhou. The bottom of the ship hit the reef and seawater poured into the cabin. It was very critical. When Lin Mo saw this, she told the villagers anxiously that the merchant ship was about to sink, and they should hurry to rescue the crew! However, everyone looked at the raging waves and dared not move forward. In the nick of time, she found some grass around her feet and threw it to the sea. Suddenly, the little blades of grass turned into large planks of fir wood and flowed to the merchant ship. Due to the attachment to the fir wood, the ship finally stopped sinking. After a while, the sea was calm and everyone on the ship thought it was the blessing from heaven and celebrated each other. When the ship got to the shore, the wood was missing. After referring to the villagers, they realized that it was Lin Mo's magical skill that had turned the grass into fir wood. And later generations called Lin Mo Mazu.

----

[1] The Chinse character of "Mo" is（默）, which means "silent".

There are countless similar legends about Mazu. In her lifetime, she gave help to people in an emergency or danger and rescued many fishing boats and merchant ships in the rough seas. What's even more touching is that she was determined not to get married, dedicating herself to doing good deeds for the world. For nearly a thousand years, people in different dynasties had given Mazu various titles more than forty times. Emperor Xianfeng ① once named Mazu as "Goddess of Heaven", with a descriptive title as long as 64 words. Before Mazu was so named and since the Emperor Song Guangzong ② named her as Linghui Goddess, Mazu had been named as Yinglie Goddess, Ciji Goddess, Puji Goddess and Cihui Goddess, etc. The folks prefer to call Mazu "Goddess of Heaven".

With the migration of Tingzhou people three hundred years ago, the worship of the Goddess of Heaven also migrated to Yunhe. The place where the Goddess of Heaven blessed also extended from the sea to the rivers and lakes. But what remains unchanged is Mazu's compassion for the people as well as her conviction of giving relief and help to all living beings.

---

① Emperor Xianfeng was the 9th emperor of the Qing Dynasty, who reigned from 1851 to 1861.

② Emperor Song Guangzong was the 12th emperor of the Song Dynasty, who reigned during February 18, 1189 to July 24, 1194.

It is for this reason that for hundreds of years, in Yunhe, where there are rivers and lakes, there is the Palace of Goddess of Heaven or Mazu Temple. When I was a child, I often learned from the elders that the Palace of Goddess of Heaven, which was built by Tingzhou people in Chishi and is now under the Yunhehu Lake, used to be full of pilgrims, and when the Goddess of Heaven's dressing was being changed every year, people would invite opera troupes to perform for three days to celebrate the huge ceremony. Now the big bell placed in Wangxiang Building on Yunhehu Lake is moved up from the palace.

There is also a Palace of Goddess of Heaven on Jiefang Street in Yunhe. It was built during the Qianlong period (1736—1795 A.D.) and used to be crowded with pilgrims. Today, the palace has been renovated under the leadership of Tong Songqing, a descendant of Tingzhou people. In addition to many visitors who go there to worship, it also becomes a place for those Tingzhou people in Yunhe to connect with each other and share homesickness.

In fact, in Yunhe's folk culture, there is not only the worship of Goddess of Heaven, but also the worship of the compassionate and helpful Goddess Ma, the worship of the respectful Goddess Flower, who saved others at the cost of her reputation, as well as the worship of Goddess Tang, who diligently assisted her father in farming and opening up wasteland. They all show that the spirit of kindness has accumulated in Yunhe's local culture.

Goddess of Heaven Temple

Marx once said, "The essence of religion is the essence of man." The folks worship culture should also be regarded as such. I think the Yunhenese worship of "goddess" in a clustered manner is essentially a worship of morality, specifically the worship of kindness such as compassion, helping others, and mutual aid. It is particularly worth mentioning that, compared to the worship of God and Allah, the worship of "goddess" who comes from the real life and was regarded as a moral incarnation is obviously more reasonable and down to earth.

It can be seen that the worship of "goddess" is a vivid proof of the word "He" (Harmony) in Yunhe in the perspective of kindness.

Folk opera culture

3.Where There Are Famous Mountains, There Are Guanyin[①] Temples in Yunhe

名山尽见观音殿

If the worship of "goddess" such as Mazu is an original native belief, then the belief in Buddhism is an acceptance of foreign belief culture. As in other parts of the country, there are many Buddhist temples in Yunhe.

At the east gate of Yunhe, along with the gentle and open Fuyun River, there is a mountain like a squatting lion-the Lion Mountain. In ancient times, the mountain once ranked first among the Eight Greatest Scenic Spots in Yunhe. There is a temple in the mountain called Puren Temple, which is known as the "Prayer

① Guanyin is a Bodhisattva in Buddhism.

184

Center in the Ten Counties of Chuzhou" [1] . Puren Temple, as the main building of the Lion Mountain, has witnessed changes throughout history. When it was rebuilt in the 14th year of Daoguang Period in the Qing Dynasty (1834 A.D.), ancient bricks of the Song Dynasty were discovered and the words "the eighth year of Jiayou period "[2] were found engraved on the bricks, which can be inferred that the temple had been there for about a thousand years. From the poems written by the literati of the past, Puren Temple was dedicated to Guanyin at that time and it once enjoyed wide reputation [3]. Coincidentally, there was also a Guanyin Hall in the famous scenic spot Huiyun Temple in Yunhe. I once chatted with Master Jifan, the abbot of Huiyun Temple, about its past and present. The abbot told me that the current Huiyun Temple, funded by many good men and women and supported by ten monks with the wish to bless all, was completed in 2007.

---

[1] Lishui was formerly called "the Ten Counties of Chuzhou". In addition to the current nine counties in Lishui, there was once a county called Xuanping, which was cancelled in 1958 and its territory was divided into the neighboring counties of Wuyi, Liandu, and Songyang.

[2] The Jiayou period was from the September of 1056 to the year 1063, which is in the Song Dynasty.

[3] Guanyin used to be called Guanshiyin, which was a free translation from the Sanskrit word "Avalokitesvar", meaning that this Bodhisattva, with great compassion, can hear all the voices from the world that need to be relieved of suffering. Later, in order to avoid the similarity to emperor' Li Shimin's name, the Bodhisattva was renamed Guanyin.

The tower of Puren Temple

According to relevant historical records, the predecessor of Huiyun Temple was "Guankeng Guanyin Temple". For three hundred years, it had been full of visitors. It can be confirmed by the folks' pet phrase "to worship Guanyin in Guankeng Village". According to legends, on the rock behind the Guanyin Temple, eagles often gathered there to listen to the Buddhist scriptures and lingered for a long time. The young and wise abbot of the temple said with a smile, "We would rather believe that the eagles are here to pray for the bless of Guanyin Bodhisattva than to insist that they are here to understand the Zen." Indeed, the Buddhism has always held the doctrine of "the equality of all life". Therefore, in the eyes of the compassionate Guanyin Bodhisattva, all sentient beings including the eagle should be sheltered and saved.

Wudai ancient road

Even more peculiar is that in the scenic areas of the famous Niutoushan Mountain, the Eight Immortals of Taoism are also associated with the Buddhist Guanyin Bodhisattva. The Niutoushan Mountain, one of the four Greatest Mountains in Yunhe, is located in the northeast of Jinshuitan Reservoir. The mountain is also the border of the county of Yunhe and Songyang. It is so named because the main peak stands high into the sky and its shape resembles a bull's head seen from the distance. According to legends, a monk built a temple dedicated to the Eight Immortals in Taoism on the Niutoushan Mountain after several years of hard work. However, the locals have always called them the Bodhisattva of Eight Immortals. And on the birthday or the enlightenment day of Guanyin Bodhisattva, worshippers are crowding in to offer flowers and incense in the temple.

In Yunhe's beautiful clouds and waters, the "worship of Guanyin", which complements the "worship of goddess" is also a beautiful scenery of Yunhe's regional culture.

Huiyun Temple

189

4.Stories About the Worship of Filial Piety and Family Love

孝子坊、百岁坊、五代同堂匾的故事

If it is to all living beings that the helpful goddess and the compassionate Guanyin Bodhisattva show kindness, then there is another kind of icon in Yunhe's folk worship culture whose kindness is towards specific individuals, such as being filial to parents, affectionate to siblings, faithful to friends and honest to strangers. As a result, the worship of filial piety, family love, faithfulness and honesty comes into being.

As in other parts of the country, there were also touching stories of dutiful sons and daughters in Yunhe's history, and there was also a place where filial piety was worshipped by future generations—Xiaozi Fang (the Memorial Archway of Filial Piety). On the west of Jiefang Street in Yunhe, there was once such a famous archway honoring the virtues of a dutiful son. The protagonist of the story is no less inferior to those in the classic stories of the *Twenty-Four Cases of Filial Piety.*

The background of this story is the rebellion of Geng Jingzhong in 1674, a general soldier of Fujian in Kangxi's reign in the Qing Dynasty. After being occupied, Yunhe was burned and plundered by the rebels who were capable of anything. A young man in Yunhe called Wang Jiajiao belled the cat and contacted some righteous people to confront the rebels. They made good use of the people's support and their familiarity with the terrain to fight against the rebels and protect the people, which frightened the rebels. After the rebels searched Wang in vain, they arrested Wang's father and imprisoned him, threatening to kill him on the other day. On hearing the news, Wang broke into the rebels' camp alone and told them that he was willing to exchange his father's freedom with his own life. He also ingeniously questioned the leader Geng Jingzhong about his name[1], "Are you righteous by threatening one's son with his father? Are you loyal to the people by rebelling for self-interest?" It is said that Geng Jingzhong was

---

[1] The leader's last name "Geng" (耿) has the meaning of "being righteous", and his first name "Jingzhong" (精忠) has the denotation of "being very loyal".

Beyond the stage

moved by Wang's courage and strong sense of righteousness and finally released the father and the son.

Later generations were moved by Wang Jiajiao's story and an archway in memory of his filial piety was built during the Yongzheng's reign of the Qing Dynasty (1723—1735 A.D.). It is said by my uncle that the archway was kept until the year of 1953, when it was demolished.

In Yunhe, there is also an archway in memory of a 100-year-old man, which was built during Daoguang's reign of the Qing Dynasty.

The protagonist of the story is Rao Yugan. It is said that at the age of 50, Rao carried a load of luggage to live with his daughter. In addition to changing clothes and other daily necessities, there were also savings he had earned for a lifetime, including land deeds, silver and jewelry. At first, his daughter and his son-in-law were quite filial, but after a period they became impatient, beginning to show disrespect to the old man.

The old man Rao Yugan couldn't bear it, so he carried his luggage home. On the way, he met a kind widow, who not only helped him carry his luggage, but also enthusiastically invited him to go to her home for tea and rest. As a result, the two fell in love. After their marriage, the loving couple not only respected each other, but also lived a happy life with lots of children and grandchildren. The old man Rao Yugan lived until the age of 100. According to the regulations promulgated by the court, the local government established a memorial archway for him, and the words "Shengping Renrui"[①] was written on it. Local people have always called it "Baisui Fang" (The Memorial Archway For People Who Live Over 100).

This quaint and elegant archway was originally at the water mouth of Ruitan Village. Due to the construction of Jinshuitan Hydropower Station, it was moved to the neighborhood of Feifeng Mountain motorway in Jinshuitan Town in 1996. It seemed a bit lonely for it to stand there alone a few years ago, but nowadays citizens, photographers and scholars can often be seen there.

In the cultural landscape of Yunhe, there is also a commemorative plaque about a family with five generations living together.

---

① "Shengping" embodies the meaning of peace and prosperity. "Renrui" refers to health and longevity. In ancient China, such archways were used as a sign of respect for the elderly.

The plaque is located in Sangling Village, Shitang Town, Yunhe County. The reason why this plaque has been talked about by the villagers is that it tells a story about the virtues of family love.

In the cultural landscape of Yunhe, there is also a commemorative plaque for a family with five generations living together.

According to research, during Kangxi's reign of the Qing Dynasty, an old man with the surname of Jiang settled down on the ancient village of Sangling with his family. Adhering to the the family's motto of being filial and living a diligent life, the descendants

View of Sangling village

of the Jiang family not only lived in harmony, but many of them also made great achievements. It's said that the Emperor Kangxi once rewarded the family's ancestor with a dragon staff as a sign of appreciation. Their later generations were quite proud. Jiang Wenchao, an old man who is also the fifth generation of the family, lived happily in a courtyard with his four generations, and the number of people living together added up to 86.

What is particularly valuable is that the offspring of Jiang Wenchao lived harmoniously, which means that there had never been a quarrel or argument, nor would they scold anyone in the family. In the 16th year of the Republic of China (1927), Zhou Fengqi, the commander of the 26th Army in Yunhe, moved by the deeds of the Jiang's family, wrote "Wushi Tongtang" (Five Generations Living Together) on a plaque as a gift to show respect to the family on Jiang Wenchao's birthday. The writer of the plaque, Zhou Fengqi, born in the late Qing Dynasty,joined "Guangfuhui"[1] after being introduced by Qiu Jin[2].

The plaque has now become a valuable and attractive sign in the ancient village of Sangling.

[1] Guangfuhui, which denotes the "restoration of China", was a famous revolutionary group founded in 1904.

[2] Qiu Jin, an advocate of feminism and pioneer of China's modern revolution, made great contributions to the Revolution of 1911.

According to relevant historical records, there were many similar archways in Yunhe that honored and promoted the virtues of filial piety and family love. It is a pity that those archways no longer exist today.

Historical vicissitudes are inevitable. The memorial archways were demolished or moved, and the plaque of the Jiang's family was once covered with dust. But it is gratifying that the kindness between people, which is the most important content in Yunhe's "He" Culture, is being passed down from generations to generations.

The Yunhe city

5.A City of Patriotism:
Loyalty and Righteousness

以忠义彰显家国情怀

If the filial piety in the virtue of kindness still seems narrow because it only refers to relatives such as parents and brothers, then the loyalty and righteousness of Yunhe people will definitely highlight the universality of their kindness. From the perspective of the relationship between the individual's home and the whole country, the essence of loyalty is the pursuit of harmony between the two, or the pursuit of harmony between the individual and the collective. Being able to sacrifice the self and serve the country with loyalty if necessary is a kind of patriotism that the Chinese has highly appreciated since ancient times.

In the city of Yunhe, patriotism is dramatically displayed during the difficult years of the War of Anti-Japanese War (1931—1945).

In December 1937, after Hangzhou was overrun by the Japanese invaders, the provincial government of Zhejiang had to migrate to the southwest of the province. The journey to the southwest by way of Longyou, Yongkang and Songyang was full of difficulties. In May 1942, the Japanese invaded the Zhejiang-Jiangxi line and the surrounding areas were in danger, so the policymakers finally decided to move to Yunhe, which was relatively remote and take it as the temporary provincial capital. Huang Shaohong, the governor of the provincial government, wrote a book entitled *Fifty Years of Memories in Yunhe* in 1945. In the book, he highly praised Yunhenese unswerving dedication and sacrifice during the national calamity.

Quite movingly, despite the fact that Yunhe people were experiencing an extremely scarce supply of materials due to a sudden increase of population, in the Spring Festival of 1945, people from all walks of life in Yunhe organized a preparatory group and mobilized the public to donate for the soldiers. Donations included pork, rice wine, rice cakes, green vegetables, chicken, duck, rice dumplings and quinine pills, etc.,

Anti-Japanese War memorial hall

which together with the fund raised added up to more than 1 million yuan. The people's strong support greatly enhanced the soldiers' determination to resist the invaders till the end.

It is worth mentioning that in the famous Fangshanling [1] Battle (1942), the brave people from all walks of life in Yunhe fought together fearlessly and provided a strong backing for our Anti-Japanese troops, which was a great contribution to defeating the Japanese invasion.

According to historical information, at the end of July 1942, the 80th division of the 22nd united team of the Japanese Army fled from Jinhua to Lishui in an attempt to invade Yunhe, the location of Zhejiang provincial government at the time. On August 2, Songyang was occupied by the Japanese aggressors, and on August 3 the Japanese troops that had entered Songyang began to attack the border between Songyang and Yunhe-Fangshanling. The frontline was more than 20 kilometers long. However, the over 1,000 invaders of the Japanese army were fired back by the Zhejiang Security Regiment.

There is a col called "Jigongji" which is 2 miles east of the Shanwangpai Village on Fangshanling. The land of Jigongji is only 400 meters above sea level and it was a must-pass for travelers

---

① A mountain ridge that lies on the border of Yunhe and Songyang.

from Yunhe to Songyang in ancient times. Due to the low terrain, the Japanese army tried to break through from Jigongji to attack Yunhe. Fortunately, the Zhejiang Security Regiment were reminded of the news by the villagers and quickly deployed new lines of defense, making good use of the trenches and bunkers to bravely fight against the enemy's aircrafts and artillery by rifles and grenades. When the battle entered a state of stalemate, people from Yunhe and the villagers nearby came to participate in the delivery of ammunition and the rescue of the wounded, and they also assisted the logistics forces to deliver meals and water timely. The battle lasted for three days and three nights. The soldiers and civilians fought against their enemies and finally repelled the aggressive Japanese invaders.

The victory of Fangshanling Battle, which was called "a small battle that determined the final" by historians, successfully prevented the Japanese aggressors from invading Yunhe, and the Japanese attempt to destroy the temporary provincial capital of Zhejiang failed, so did their vicious ambition to disintegrate the fighting spirit of the soldiers and the civilians in Zhejiang.

The patriotism of the city is also engraved in the historical memory of Xiaoshun Arsenal.

In April 1938, Huang Shaohong, the governor of Zhejiang Province, decided to move the iron factory that had been in the south of Hangzhou to Xiaoshun Village to produce rifles, machine guns, bullets and grenades. That was because the Xiaoshun Village in Yunhe was a place which was convenient in transportation and easy to defend. In just a few years, the arsenal named Zhejiang Iron Factory grew rapidly. It set up three branch factories nearby and the number of workers grew from over 1,000 to more than 4,000. The number of machines also increased from about 30 to more than 1,000. By the year of 1942, the arsenal was able to produce more than 1,000 rifles, 50 light machine guns and 60,000 grenades per month. The weapons and ammunition not only met the needs for the Anti-Japanese War in Zhejiang Province, but were also transported to other places to contribute to the national Anti-Japanese war.

As the largest arsenal in Zhejiang during the Anti-Japanese War, the number of workers in Xiaoshun Arsenal was up to thousands. The number of Yunhe workers at that time could not be examined in detail, but it must be a lot. When I was in Yunhe High School in 1975, my deskmate was from Xinhua Factory, a third-tier military factory. Its main product was rifles. At that time, my deskmate was very proud that his parents were workers who produced guns. However, a student from the next-door class said more proudly, "My grandfather produced machine guns in Xiaoshun before!" Everyone, including me, did not believe it at first, but our history teacher Wang Gongdu affirmed the fact.

In fact, from the perspective of experts studying the history of the Anti-Japanese War in Lishui, a greater contribution that Yunhe people had made to the arsenal was their logistical support. According to the book *An Oral History of the Anti-Japanese War in Lishui*, due to the increase of workers in the arsenal at that time, the housing problem was extremely serious. The kind and righteous villagers in Xiaoshun even vacated their family's ancestral halls for emergency.

With the construction of Shitang Reservoir, the arsenal is now sunk under the water. But the contributions Yunhe people had made to the arsenal will not be erased by time.

Indeed, the patriotism of Yunhe people which is the manifestation of the virtue of kindness is not only reflected in the period of the Anti-Japanese War.

In the 1960s, China decided to design and build Xin'anjiang Hydropower Station on its own. A large population of people in the reservoir areas of Chun'an [1] and Jiande [2] needed to be resettled. And Yunhe became an important place for those migrants. During the fifty years, the migrants married the natives, shared customs and started business in Yunhe, living harmoniously with the locals just like family members.

---

[1] A county located in the hilly mountains in the western part of Zhejiang Province.

[2] A county located in the west of Zhejiang Province.

Today'squiet and peaceful Xiaoshun

Spring in the countryside   Back home for the new year

    I remember when I was having a meal in the cafeteria of Zhejiang University, I accidentally heard a professor of physics talked on the phone in native Yunhe dialect. I excitedly greeted him with the same language. It turned out that he had been living in Yunhe until he was admitted to the Department of Physics of the former Hangzhou University. His father was from Chun'an and migrated to Meiyuan, Yunhe. He said that the best memory of his childhood was that his mother, a native Yunhenese,

206

fried Jianxue① and Youtongbing② for the whole family. He added that the warmest memory was his mother patiently teaching his grandma how to make Shanmaci③ as well as sweet potatoes chips and persimmon cakes.

Time passed and the same problem of migration occurred in Yunhe. Due to the construction of Jinshuitan Hydropower Station in 1978, a large number of residents in the reservoir area of Yunhe had to leave their homeland.

---

① A representative snack of Yunhe. Jianxue is mashed sweet potatoes with glutinous rice and water, which was then fried in deep oil as a mixture. Jianxue is in the shape of small cylinder and tastes crispy in the outside but soft and glutinous inside. The golden-colored dim-sum is an essential snack for urban and rural residents in Yunhe during the Spring Festival.

② Youtongbing is also a representative snack of Yunhe. It is cakes made of shredded pumpkin or radish mixed with flour, which is then placed in an iron vessel and fried in deep oil. The snack tastes crispy and refreshing.

③ Shanmaci, which is made from the leaf juice of a shrub, is also known as "Green Tofu" or "Guanyin Tofu". It is clear as crystals and can be cooked in soup or enjoyed as a cold dish. It not only tastes soft and fresh, but also has some medical effect according to Chinese traditional medical science.

Dried sweet potato slices

My uncle's family were those residents who were then placed in a rather remote place in Huzhou City-Miaoxi. When we met shortly after their migration, my cousin told me that the desolateness of Miaoxi was really beyond their imagination. But the folks who migrated from Yunhe with them did not complain. Instead, they quickly settled down there with hard work. My cousin's eldest daughter became a technical expert of the local silk factory after graduation, and later she became the deputy director responsible for techniques. The younger daughter of my cousin was admitted to Zhejiang University and was recommended to be a PhD due to her excellent academic performance, which made her the second PhD student in our hometown Chishi.

The touching stories of the Jinshuitan migrants who had sacrificed their homes for the development of the country was once reported by CCTV News. My cousin told me that when their family watched TV that night, their eyes stared at the screen, full of excited tears.

This is the patriotism within Yunhe people.

aking sweet green rice balls

6.The Modernization and Innovation of Kindness

和善之德的现代传承与弘扬光大

From accepting the She people who migrated more than a thousand years ago to being kind to the migrants who came from the reservoir areas of China's first self-designed hydropower stations, from actively participating in the battlefield of Anti-Japanese War to moving out from the Jinshuitan Hydropower Station to start new life with hard work , from the stories about the memorial archway of filial piety and family love to the Xiaoshun Arsenal···The residents of Yunhe have established countless historical monuments of harmony and kindness.

More importantly, in the city the tradition of "He" (Harmony) Culture is not only inherited in modern times, but is constantly being innovated.

For example, the "Mr. Li Help Group" with the purpose of "helping others and being happy" has more than 4,000 registered volunteers. Its unpaid service covers almost all areas of people's life, and it has become a representative display of the city's kindness.

Ye Shiyun, known as the "Faithful Orphan", spent six years from the age of eleven paying off all debts his parents had owed by recycling waste materials for money, working part-time, and saving salvage fund, which is the most vivid chapter about the virtue of faithfulness in contemporary Yunhe.

Liao Weiping, an employee of the Water Affairs Group, known as "the Most Beautiful Nightwalker", spent countless nights walking in the streets and alleys with a "listening stick" in his hands, guarding the water safety of the entire county.

Zhong Huayan, a PE teacher of the Third Middle School of Yunhe, who is called "Sister of Swallow" by her students, has spent most of her holidays with the children since she formed the "Cloud Dream" calisthenics team. Under her guidance her team of rural teenagers even appeared on the stage of "China Dream Show".

More examples are like:

He Shangqing, a well-known entrepreneur who created the legend of wooden toys with the basic business philosophy of "harmony and faithfulness";

Chen Keyun, an enterprise manager who actively assists poor students and disabled people;

Jin Jianzhong, a village cadre who gave up his city life and went back home to serve the villagers;

Chen Zigui, a rural doctor who appears at the patients' side at any time of the day;

Pan Limin, who has overcome the shortage of staff and funding to make great contributions to the work of ancient books in Yunhe Library;

Lan Xiangmei, an ordinary villager who has been taking care of her parents-in-law and brother-in-law for 30 years;

Feng Jianhong and Xu Dongdong, who regardless of their personal safety rescued three children fallen into the water;

Mao Zhengwei, an employee of Rural Credit Cooperatives who rushed into the sea of fire and rescued an old man at the risk of his own life;

"FU" (blessing) on the door

Ye Shihai, who takes a tramp home and treats him like a family member…

I believe that if you write down these practitioners of kindness one by one, it will be a long list.

If the stories of these benevolent people are just learned from the news reports, then the next stories are my personal experience. The protagonists of the following stories are my three class head teachers.

When I transferred from Chishi Primary School to Guixi Primary School, my new head teacher had a very elegant name:

Pan Jinluan. At that time, our school had a committee that managed affairs related to the poor and lower-middle peasants. This was the highest authority of the school in that era. In the eyes of the committee members, knowledge from the book was not worth learning. The most important lessons were about industrial and agricultural production as well as military affairs. But our teacher Ms.Pan, often took opportunities to call us back from the field to the classroom for the sake of knowledge learning. She has a pet phrase, "You will regret it if you don't take classes seriously!"

Once, maybe because of playfulness, only a few students of the whole class returned to school. Ms. Pan still gave us lessons very seriously. Many years later, Gaokao (the National College Entrance Examination) was restored and three of us from the primary class entered undergraduate programs, and I got the first place in liberal arts in our county that year. You know, that is the year 1979 when only eight of the high school graduates in the county were admitted to the undergraduate programs, and our Guixi Primary School was just a rural school.

The head teacher of my junior high school is Wei Yuanxian. Born in a family of scholars, she taught at the same school after graduation because of her outstanding academic performance. Perhaps Ms. Wei was so excellent herself that she set strict requirements on students. I remember there was a teacher named Yan Li[①] in charge of our school, and his name stands for "being strict" in Chinese, but everyone said that our head teacher Ms. Wei was "stricter than 'the strict'".

But it was such a strict head teacher that shed tears when she saw my knees injured at the sports meeting. On the contrary, I comforted my head teacher, "Anyway, I won the first place for our class." Ms. Wei waved her hands and told me decisively that she would rather not have had the first place!

When I was in the first year of high school my head teacher was Wu Aiping. Ms. Wu taught us Chinese. Because of the importance of Chinese composition in Gaokao, our school organized a school-wide composition competition, and I won the first place in the group of freshmen, which made me very proud for some time.

---

① The name "Yan Li" share the same pronunciation and character with the word "being strict" in Chinese.

In a summer vacation twenty years later, I went back to my alma mater to participate in the class reunion. On a very occasional situation, I learned that when the teachers discussed the winning list that year, they were more inclined to recommend Ms. Wu's daughter Xu Wei. But Ms. Wu, who was present, strongly opposed it. Her reason was that she had just aroused my interest in composition and my enthusiasm must be protected. As for her child, she said that she could help and train her daughter anytime and anywhere.

Many years later, I was invited to give a series of talks on Hangzhou TV. When we were recording the episode for the Teacher's Day, I told stories about my three head teachers quiet affectionately. My recording assistant, a senior student at Communication University of Zhejiang, said with tears in her eyes, "Professor, you are so fortunate!" Later, the producer told me that the episode had won great popularity after being broadcasted.

In the city of Yunhe, it's not just the teachers' kindness that moved me.

On a summer night in 1974, I was so naughty that I fell from the third floor of the dining hall in my father's factory, and I lost my consciousness. After finally getting through the emergency call of the county's hospital, my father was told that the hospital's only ambulance was out. The neighbors who heard the news said nothing but borrowed a tricycle which was used for buying groceries for the factory's dining hall. My three neighbors, one in the front riding the tricycle and the others both pushing from the two sides, rushed to the hospital. I was in a coma lying in my father's arms on the tricycle, knowing nothing about it. After that, every time I heard my father describe the moving scene of that night, feelings of appreciation welled up in my heart.

This is the kindness between neighbors in the city of Yunhe.

In the winter of 1979, a rare heavy snow occurred in southern Zhejiang. The long-distance shuttle bus I took from Jinhua to Yunhe was blocked at Lishui Station because of the road closure. Looking at the sky, I estimated that the snow wouldn't stop soon. Longing for home, I decided to walk home with a companion whom I had just met in the station. After walking for a whole day, we got to Xikou Village in the evening, which was more than 5 kilometers away from downtown Yunhe.My companion's home was just in the village so he warmly invited me to rest at his house before leaving. What impressed me was that his parents not only entertained me with a warm meal, but also invited me to stay for the night to ensure the following long walk. The next day, the hospitable host boiled an egg for me as food supply on the road.

This is people's kindness to strangers in the city of Yunhe.

In 2017, my father, who unfortunately had suffered from Alzheimer's disease for eight years, was in a deep coma. When my brother and I were at a loss, it was the doctor Qiu Yunwei in Yunhe Integrated TCM and Western Medicine Hospital who gave us a helping hand in time and resolutely accepted my old father. Doctor Qiu and his colleagues tried their best to alleviate my father's suffering during the dying period. My father appeared particularly calm and serene when he died.

This is the kindness of the medical workers in the city of Yunhe.

In the summer of 2019, due to the need for research on Yunhe's "He" Culture, our group went to many places, including the mountains and countryside. Once, our car went dead unexpectedly on the way to Longmen. After searching on the phone, we found there was a repair shop in the nearby town of Jinshuitan. I hurriedly let someone ask for help. Soon a young repairman came. He opened the hood and got the car repaired soon. When we were about to pay, he waved his hand and said, "It's just a little problem. I will be sorry if you pay me." Watching him leaving on his electric bicycle, we could do nothing but say "thank you" to express our gratitude.

This is the kindness of the self-employed individuals in the city of Yunhe.

What's more, I also want to write about the kindness of the officials in Yunhe.

In terms of the administrative theories, the kindness of officials is good governance. As a beautiful "scenery" of goodwill, the officials' performance in good governance in Yunhe have always been well received. During our investigation and visits, our research group found that they deserved the honor. Whether it is the county's party secretary or the village cadres, the officials in Yunhe work hard on taking good care of the natural resources, solving the problems of people's life, and reconstructing the old parts of the city, which reveals their dedication to staying true to their original aspiration.

Yunhe Terraces in spring

Ren Shunv, the "Secretary of Yunhe Terraces", is a good example. When she came to Yunhe as the Secretary of the County Committee of the CPC, she decided to make tourism as a starting point to help Yunhe's economy reach a new level. In the meantime, she managed to make Yunhe Terraces get admitted as an AAAA National Tourist Attraction [1] . Because she kept going to the ministries and commissions concerned in Beijing to report and communicate about the relevant issues, the people there called her "Secretary of Yunhe Terraces".

Another example is "the Father of Yunhe Masters" -Wang Xinrong. In the 1980s and 1990s, some talented Yunhe farmers went to Jiangxi, Hubei and other provinces in China to engage in the cultivation and sales of edible fungi. This triggered the inspiration of Wang Xinrong, who was in charge of the related affairs. He started working on the promotion of the project of "Yunhe Masters". Nowadays, "Yunhe Masters" not only make profits themselves, but also greatly promote the development of the local economy. "Yunhe Masters" has been reported by national media including CCTV for many times.

---

[1] According to the quality classification of tourist attractions in the People's Republic of China, scenic areas are divided into five levels. From high to low are AAAAA, AAAA, AAA, AA, and A.

Ma Guohua, "the Mayor of Wooden Toys", is also a representative. As the main industry of the county, Yunhe Wooden Toys has now become famous at home and abroad. Some media once reported that, "In the poetic landscapes of Yunhe, a stunning wooden toy industry was born." As the vice mayor of the county at the time, Ma Guohua dedicated himself to the promotion of the wooden toy industry. It is because of these efforts he had made that he not only won the reputation of "the Mayor of Wooden Toys", but was also elected as the Emeritus Chairman of Yunhe Wooden Toy Association.

Lin Shaoqing, the "Secretary of Chestnuts", is another good example. When he was the Secretary of the CPC committee of Shitang Town, he found that the villagers' life was too hard. He thought that if the chestnuts were planted in the mountains, then it would be a practical way to help the villagers get rid of poverty and become rich without destroying the natural environment. It has always been his style to do what he says, so he achieved the goal of building a 10,000-acre chestnut base in only three years by mobilizing the villagers, attracting investment, and encouraging the Forestry Bureau to become a shareholder.

Products of geographical indication:
Yunhe pears and black fungus

It can be said with certainty that if we list the active practitioners of good governance in the city of Yunhe one by one, it will also be a long list.

When it comes to the good governance in this city, there is a detail worth mentioning. After reporting to Ye Bojun, the Secretary of the County Committee of the CPC, on the progress of our project, I showed several graduate students who came to Yunhe for the first time around the government hall, which looked somewhat weathered. When our group walked back to the hotel where we were staying, the dusk was deepening and the city lights started to blaze, which made the street view really attractive. At this time, one of the students sighed, "Compared with the old desks in the county secretary's office, the city of Yunhe looks much more beautiful."

As a native, I followed the topic and introduced the history of the county to the students. The downtown of Yunhe was originally located in Ruoxi Town, which was named after a river. Then it was renamed Chengguan Town after the People's Republic of China was founded. I remember when I was studying in Yunhe Middle

Yunhe ancient street

School in the 1970s, my geography teacher Zhu Zuocheng told us a folk ballad describing Yunhe County. I still remember the lyrics clearly, which goes that "*three tofu stores are on the street; You cry your tofu at the end of the street, and I hear it in the remotest corner.*" The ballad vividly depicts the old town of Yunhe, which covered only a small area with sparse stores.

Now, dramatic changes have taken place in Yunhe. Under the guidance of the Yunhe government, people work together and finally the pattern of "A Big City Born in A Small County" [①] has achieved great results. Although the county's total population is only 114,000, 80% of Yunhe people live in the urban areas and 93.4% of the students get educated in urban schools. Besides, 96% of the enterprises develop in the urban areas of the county. The urbanization rate of Yunhe reaches 69.6%. This development strategy is praised by the academia as a new model of "the urbanization of mountainous areas". More importantly, it also makes people have a sense of fulfillment and happiness by taking part in and interacting with the city's development.

---

① It's a policy carried out by the Yunhe government that focuses on the county's urbanization and development.

Prepare for the new year

More hopefully, in the post "A Big City Born in A Small County" era, Yunhe is actively working to complete the new mission of making the county a new model of the new-type urbanization for mountainous areas across the country.

We have reasons to believe that in the future Yunhe County will definitely show her grace in a smarter, more livable, and more beautiful way.

The new county

Conclusion

结束语

After we give the cultural interpretation of the word "He" in the two dimensions, which refers to the harmony between man and nature and the harmony between the individuals and others. We are able to propose a city slogan based on such thinking, and that is "*Wonderland of Clouds and Waters; City of Harmony and Kindness*". "Wonderland of Clouds and Waters" presents the "harmony" between man and nature, while "City of Harmony and Kindness" highlights the "harmony" between individuals and others.

As we all know, the Chinese "He" Culture has a very long history. According to the research of experts, the word "He" is among the earliest Chinese characters that appeared in the ancient bronze inscriptions. What's more, "He" is always treasured by Chinese traditional culture. It is summed up in President Xi Jinping's speech on May 15, 2014 at the 60th Anniversary of the founding of Chinese People's Association for Friendship with Foreign Countries: The "He" Culture in China has a long history, and it contains a world view that holds the unity of heaven and man, an international outlook that believes in the coexistence of all in harmony, a social outlook that insists on "harmony but no uniformity" and a moral concept that believes in the goodness of man.

Based on the theory of Chinese traditional "He" Culture, we have carried out a cultural interpretation of the word "He" of Yunhe in the two dimensions that covers the harmonious relationship between man and nature and the harmonious relationship between individuals and others, which is not only an implementation of president Xi Jinping's spirit in his speech about China's "He" Culture, but also a practical effort to build cultural confidence in a specific region.

Some scholars once conducted a big data analysis on The *Yongle Canon* [1] , a magnificent classic of Chinese culture. They found that the book involves more than 40,000 Chinese characters, and the character "He" (和) is one of the most-frequently-used in the 10,000 commonly-used characters. Coincidentally, Yunhe is also a "1 in 10000" place. Because its area and population are both one ten thousandth of the country. The coincidence added a bit of pride and a sense of mission to our team members on the research of Yunhe's "Harmony" Culture.

We firmly believe that under the leadership of the County Committee of CPC and the county government, and through the active participation of Yunhe people, the new generations of Yunhenese can not only inherit the "He" Culture, but will certainly carry it forward and further develop it under new historical conditions, which can provide an important spiritual impetus for the construction of "A Big City Born in A Small County" as well as the effort to turn Yunhe into a model of new-type urbanization for mountainous areas across the country.

---

[1] "The Yongle Canon", compiled by 2,000 scholars and completed in 1408, A.D., was the world's earliest and biggest encyclopedia, which contains 22,937 volumes bound in 11,095 books with a total of 370 million Chinese characters.

Riverside garden

Postscript

后记

Today, no one should question that "He" (Harmony) has become the most appropriate logo and cultural identification code for Yunhe. In other words, just as Jiande explores the"De"(Morality) Culture, Jiashan the "Shan" (Goodness) Culture, and Cixi the "Ci" (Loving)[①] Culture, it is surely appropriate for Yunhe to propose the "He" Culture as the city's core value and cultivate and develop it. This is not only because the ancestors left us descendants with the wonderful name of "Yunhe", but also due to the valuable practical explorations that have been made on the "He" (Harmony) Culture by people from all walks of life under the active leadership of the County Committee of the CPC and the county government.

---

① Jiande, Jiashan and Cixi are all cities in Zhejiang Province.

Therefore I believe that the essence of Yunhe's spirit, the conception of city slogan, the design of the city logo, and the construction of the city's cultural brand should all be based on the word "He" (Harmony), which should be a consensus that is no longer controversial. What we have to do is to further, explore, interpret or promote the "He" (Harmony) Culture.

It is for this reason that I sincerely hope that my personal interpretation of the "Harmony Culture" of Yunhe in this book can contribute to the improvement of the city's reputation.

Finally, I would like to thank Ye Bojun [1], Lin Jianwen [2] and Chen Jingyi [3] for their care and guidance in the research. I would also send my gratitude to Dr. Zhu Xiaohong and other members of the research team for their hard work. In addition, the efforts that Zhou Lingli [4] has made in the English translation should also be appreciated. I believe it will play a positive role in promoting the story of our Yunhe's "Harmony" Culture abroad.

For the postscript.

Zhang Yinghang

January 28, 2020

Fuyun Community, Yunhe

① The Secretary of the Yunhe County Committee of the CPC.

② Minister of the Propaganda Department of Yunhe Committee of the CPC.

③ Vice Minister of the Propaganda Department of Yunhe Committee of the CPC.

④ A teacher in Lishui Vocational and Technical College.

〔 云 水 佳 境 是 故 乡 〕

文一作品 · 二〇二〇年秋